Desert Bonds

A Father and Son's Middle East Odyssey

Twenty two days in Lebanon, Syria, Jordan, Israel & Palestine 2024

Edited by Yvonne Reddin and Peter Murtagh.
Design and layout by Eimear D'Arcy. Cover design by 2funkidesign.
Published in Ireland by Orla Kelly Publishing.

Photographs are produced with acknowledgment/permission of Denis Dwyer and Dermod Dwyer, with some Syria images from Erin Coyle and Francesca Lupec.

P216/217: Wikipedia/Vatican Press/ shrbm75: Holy Fire image.

Map by Darren Bennett, www.dkbcreative.com and image:
Spirit of Adventure painting by artist Niall Leavy www.niallleavy.com.

Orla Kelly Publishing, 27 Kilbrody, Mount Oval, Rochestown, Cork.

Barry Design and Print, 34 Eastgate Dr, Wallingstown, Co. Cork.

REVIEWS

"The trip in itself embodies relentless optimism about what is possible, tempered with brutal realism about what it takes to bring the possible to fruition... their greatest gift is in sharing their experience and reflections with us in this book."
Marty Linsky – international bestselling author on Leadership, media commentator, and Adjunct Professor at Harvard University

"Dermod and Denis Dwyer show their humanity and curiosity in this remarkable travel book, a journey into the humanity behind the conflicts that continue to this day, in one of the most beautiful areas of the world."
Áine Lawlor – Irish radio and television broadcaster (RTÉ)

"Part travelogue, part history, and part adventure, Desert Bonds is above all about the connections forged between a father, son, and the people they meet. It is a revealing story about the central place of the Middle East today and our history and the connections forged between a father, son, and the people they meet. Rich in detail, fascinating and very human."
Tom Lyons – Business Journalist of the year (2011, 2016, and 2018), editorial positions in The Sunday Times, Irish Times, Sunday Business Post, author, and co-founder and CEO of the Currency.

"If you think you know the Middle East, if you think its problems can be reduced to one dimensional 'good guys' and 'bad guys', then you have not been there or listened sufficiently to its various voices. Dermod and Denis' foray into Lebanon, Syria, Jordan and Israel had them do just that. What emerges in this account of their adventure is a taste of the colour, the complexity, the ancient history, shared and contested, and the equally ancient enmities, that make the region so fascinating, so beguiling... and so very dangerous. Credit to them too for inviting some of the people they met to be part of the project by writing their own contributions. Beautifully illustrated, this is a story of resilience and of hope."
Peter Murtagh – Journalist and author (From Tip to Top, Buen Camino; Gill Books).

"It is a quick-moving, very descriptive story introducing us to a fascinating array of people, cultures, situations, and places. The maps, pictures and illustrations are amazing."
Declan O'Sullivan – Author (When Is The Tide Turning?)

"We fear the unknown, we fear violence and we fear death, but Dermod and Denis Dwyer face up to all three in their journey through the Middle East. A place where so many fear being judged for their beliefs and actions. Dermod and Denis do not judge but they do reveal, and in the process help our understanding of a huge tragedy."
William Micklem – Bestselling author, coach. international speaker and influencer with over 1 million followers on TEDx Talk

"Desert Bonds goes beyond being a mere travelogue recounting a hugely memorable and often moving father-and-son trip through one of the most sensitive parts of the world. It is full of awareness about the complexity of people and place, as the authors made it their business to find out what lies behind the harrowing conflicts in Israel-Palestine, Syria and Lebanon, and were received with warm hospitality wherever they went by people whose chief characteristic is extraordinary resilience"
Frank McDonald – Author and Irish Times journalist

"A father and son journey through troubled places in troubled times finds humanity, resilience and hope in the middle of geopolitical madness."
Brian Byrne – Journalist, publisher, and podcaster

"I felt like I went on a Geography and History journey learning so much about this part of the world. Dermod and Denis certainly set the scene for each place they visited and the people they met along the way which humanised such a complex conflict zone. The maps and photos show the extraordinarily beautiful landscapes they visited and travelled through. This book is for anyone who wants to learn about different cultures, resilience and the people who live there and delight in seeing visitors come to their countries, towns and villages. It instils a message of hope for the future of humankind."
Yvonne Reddin – Travel writer, journalist and author

"With a deep awareness of history and politics and of the fortitude and hospitality encountered in the turbulent Middle East, this unique journal features a rich array of vignettes which fascinate. A homage both to adventurous spirits and to a father-son relationship."
Micheal O'Siadhail – Internationally acclaimed Irish poet

To Helen – for selfless encouragement and boundless love, and for our respective families present and those who have left us – all part of our story and interwoven tapestry.

Travel leaves you speechless.
Then it turns you into a storyteller.

Ibn Battuta – Arab scholar and explorer

CONTENTS

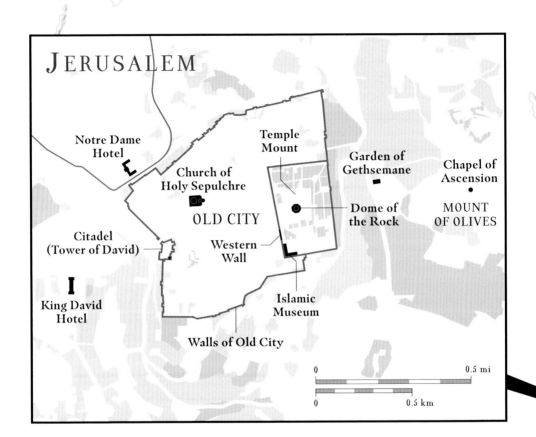

Rhodes

Alanya

JERUSALEM

Notre Dame
Hotel

Temple
Mount

Garden of
Gethsemane

Chapel of
Ascension

Church of
Holy Sepulchre

OLD CITY

Dome of
the Rock

MOUNT
OF OLIVES

Citadel
(Tower of David)

Western
Wall

King David
Hotel

Islamic
Museum

Walls of Old City

| 0 | | 0.5 mi |

| 0 | | 0.5 km |

Matrouh

Alexandria

Port
Said

EGYPT

CAIRO

Su

II

Qarun
Lake

Nile

| 0 | 20 | 40 | 60 | 80 | 100 mi |

| 0 | 50 | 100 | 150 | 200 km |

Iskenderun

Aleppo

Euphrates

*Lake
Assad*

NICOSIA

imassol

Hama

Al Wadi

Krak des
Chevaliers

Homs

SYRIA

Palmyra

Tripoli

Byblos

Our Lady of Lebanon

Jeita

BEIRUT

Chateau Ksara

Bekaa
Valley

Mt. Lebanon

Temple of Baalbek

Maaloula

Aanjar   Jubb'adin

DAMASCUS

LEBANON

Jordan

ranean

a

Capharnum

Haifa

Nazareth

GOLAN
HEIGHTS

Sea of Galilee

Tiberius

ISRAEL

Ben Gurion Airport

Tel Aviv

JERUSALEM

Ein Karim

Ashkelon

Gaza

AZA STRIP

Rafah

Jarash

WEST
BANK

Al-Maghtas

AMMAN

Mt. Nebo

Madaba

Allenby Border
Crossing

Yad
Vashem

Bethlehem

Dead Sea

JORDAN

Little Petra

Petra

*Sinai
Desert*

SAUDI
ARABIA

III

WADI
RUM

Aqaba

INTRODUCTION AND BACKGROUND

April 16 – May 8, 2024

We – Denis and I – are the storytellers of this journey.

It took us, in April and May 2024, through the heart of the Middle East. It led us into the Old Levant, through parts of Lebanon, Syria, Jordan, and Israel, including the tense area near the Erez Gaza border crossing at the northern end of the Gaza Strip. From the Israeli border kibbutzim to the Sea of Galilee we navigated the region that is rich in history and complexity.

We write about the people we met, the moments we shared and the deep-rooted cultural and religious ties we encountered. Our story is set against the backdrop of a geopolitical landscape that shifts, depending on where you stand. We share personal experiences – getting lost in the bustling streets of Beirut, dancing in Aleppo and in Damascus, watching the sun set over the Dead Sea, breaking bread with Ethiopian pilgrims, witnessing the Orthodox Easter Holy Fire ceremony and attending the solemn Yad Vashem Holocaust Remembrance Day in Jerusalem.

We listened to heart-breaking stories from those who have lived amidst conflict and violence on all sides. The fact that our visit was in the aftermath of the murderous October 7, 2023 Hamas incursion into Israel, and Israel's retaliatory war in Gaza, only sharpened our awareness of the region's deep-seated tensions and volatility. Everywhere we went, we met people whose lives had been transformed by unpredictable twists of fate. Some families we encountered had been torn apart, while others managed to maintain a semblance of normalcy despite the turmoil around them. Yet, no matter where we travelled, we were greeted with warmth and hospitality.

We came home to Ireland in awe of the resilience of those we met, but carrying with us also their fears that what was, at that time, limited conflict could ignite into something far worse, engulfing what remains of their homes and lives. Tragically, since then those fears have since become a reality.

Poignantly, although the region through which we travelled is the epicentre of key world religions and historic roots, there is a sense that it is diminished in its strategic relevance in the new geopolitical Gulf-centred Middle East. It's no longer seen as important militarily, politically or as a source for future natural resources. Unfortunately, it has become a proxy theatre for regional and global powers to flex their influence at a safe distance.

This book is a distilled compilation taken from our experiences of daily life in the region while we were there. We wrote daily recollections and took many photos. We have also logged inputs from some of the friends we made and people we encountered along our journey.

Days before we left Ireland – the Iranian embassy in Damascus was bombed by the Israeli Air Force resulting in all commercial air traffic in the region being suspended. By a stroke of luck on the day we were due to fly, air travel, to and within the region, miraculously resumed. Synchronicity, perhaps.

Dermod and Denis Dwyer
Greystones and Wicklow Town, January 2025

'The Spirit of Adventure' by Irish artist Niall Leavy

BACKGROUND AND PREPARATION

April 16th, 2024

On board the Turkish Airlines flight from Dublin to Beirut, Denis and I began a journey into four Middle East countries. At that time each was classed by governments and insurance companies as 'hostile environments'. But we were not to be deterred. We made all our own arrangements after we had previously booked a seven-day trip to Syria in early September 2023.

I had visited Syria and Jordan briefly, professionally, over 30 years earlier. I had been reading *Into Iraq*, Michael Palin's book about his 2022 trip to the region, and it reignited my interest. Palin first wanted to visit Syria but his plans were stymied at the last minute by the Syrian authorities based on a donation he had made previously to an aid agency. He and his film crew chose instead to travel to Iraq.

I contacted Untamed Borders, an adventure travel company specialising in guided tours to remote destinations. They offer unique and immersive experiences in some of the world's most challenging but culturally rich regions. Palin's film crew had used Untamed Borders to make their ground arrangements. The company was founded in 2008 and are travel *fixers* who help journalists and other adventure travellers to visit hard-to-reach places in the Middle East. As Palin put it, Untamed Borders specialise 'taking people to places most other people don't want to go'.

When we first inquired in September 2023, Untamed Borders had just announced plans for a single small group trip to Syria, set to begin on April 20, 2024. We immediately booked our spots and then filled out our itinerary with visits to other countries in the region. Lebanon was a natural addition, and Jordan, right next door, also made perfect sense. With long-term friends in Israel, I hoped we could also include it in our journey. At that time, the region was relatively calm.

Since the post-Arab Spring civil war of 2011, Syria had become a pariah state under heavy international sanctions, with travel strongly discouraged by the European Union, United States and most other nations. Despite the challenges, Denis and I each took on planning responsibilities. I managed the logistics, while Denis, juggling work and projects, delved into the history. He likely saw this as a far-fetched idea, humouring his ageing father with what seemed like an unlikely adventure. As the situation in the region deteriorated from the October 2023 Hamas attack, the trip did indeed seem improbable.

The Irish Department of Foreign Affairs (DFA) issued bulletins to discourage Irish citizens travelling to these troubled areas. The UK, USA and most EU countries did the same. Before we left Ireland, we registered with the DFA, notifying them of our plans to visit Lebanon, Syria, Jordan and perhaps Israel. Our response was acknowledged, and we were advised to keep them updated. We did.

Before we could finally commit to our journey, we had an insurance dilemma. One of Untamed Borders' conditions for taking us to Syria was that we had full insurance cover, preferably to include kidnapping and/or personal extraction.

We had VHI worldwide travel insurance which, not surprisingly, excluded cover for Lebanon, Syria, Jordan and Israel. Finally, I found a professional travel link to another international broker, IATI. They offered global cover insurance including Lebanon, Syria and Jordan but not for Israel. I shared with my Israeli friend that we couldn't get insurance for his country. He replied, 'That's ridiculous. Don't worry we will get you covered in Israel'.

I hope this book, filled with photographs and maps, captures the essence of our journey through these 'hostile environments'. It's important to emphasise that our focus is solely on the places we visited, without attempting to connect regions or delve into geopolitical complexities beyond our perspective as genuine tourists – we are not journalists. Some countries naturally feature more prominently than others, as we spent varying amounts of time in each. Given its central role in the region, it's no surprise that Israel occupies a larger part of our story.

Denis's thoughts before travelling:

In the months before we were due to leave, I had very mixed feelings about the trip. I was hugely curious about the opportunity to visit such fascinating lands, but I was also nervous as I didn't want us to be reckless or for others to be worried about us. And I didn't know whether it was appropriate for us to visit Israel given the indiscriminate killings in Gaza we were seeing on the news and the disproportionate nature of the Israeli response to the horrific Hamas attacks on 7 October 2023 when 1,200 Israelis were killed and over 200 taken hostage. And yet... if we didn't go now, we would never go... we both love history and experiencing new cultures, so why not?

Dad, like me, is interested in exploration and adventures, and I admired his courage in wanting to undertake such a trip. It would be a journey across countries and cultures, and through history, while also adding a new chapter in our own father and son story.

My wife Helen's thoughts on our adventure:

Even my wife, Helen, was sceptical, but supportive. 'If you want to go, please go ahead,' she told me. 'It's a unique opportunity for the two of you to have a special trip together – father and son together time.'

And so our journey begins.

LEBANON

Republic of Lebanon

الجمهورية اللبنانية (Arabic)

al-Jumhūrīyah al-Lubnānīyah

French: Liban

Preparing for takeoff

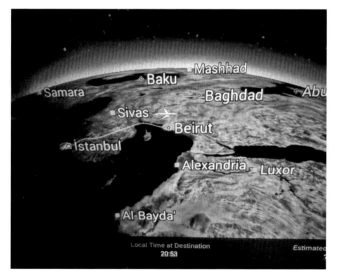

Flight map

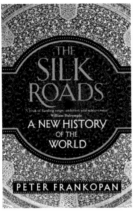

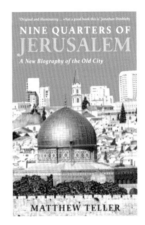

Travel reading

Tuesday, April 16th, just a week after Easter, Denis and I boarded Turkish Airlines flight TK826 to Istanbul with an onward connection to Beirut, Lebanon. As we checked in our bags at Dublin Airport, the airline agent asked us to stand aside. She phoned the airline head office in Istanbul to ask if she was allowed to check our bags through to Beirut. Her action was prompted, undoubtedly, by the fatal bombing attack the previous week on the Iranian consulate in the Syrian capital, Damascus when all commercial flights were banned from the airspace of war-torn Lebanon, Syria, Jordan, Iran and Israel. Thankfully, our bags went straight through. In the airport shopping area, I bought two Irish flags in case we needed to indicate our nationality. Pinned inside my backpack was the Angel of Joy – a safe journey gift from Denis's roommate Annie. We took off for the five-hour flight to Istanbul, Turkey's largest city, known for centuries as Constantinople, which straddles the Bosporus strait between Europe and Asia.

We had a layover of almost three hours in the city's vast new $26 billion dollar airport that only opened in 2019. I took a selfie at the terminal's Islamic history display, with the words from the Holy Quran (20:114) which read, 'Say; O my Lord! Advance me in knowledge.'

Denis thought the airport 'was gleaming, a stunning design'.

'The modern scientific method was first established in Islamic civilisation'

We sat in a café beside an exhibition dedicated to Islamic scientists from the Golden Age of Islam, taking it all in.

Lebanon's complex power sharing system was recently described by the France 24 international news company as the 'Cause of all ills' made up as it is by peoples with diverse religious belief – Druze, Maronite Christians, Sunni Muslims, Hezbollah and Shi'ite Muslims. The leaders of each are warlords turned politicians power sharing amid other unlikely partnerships. Lebanon suffered from the almost never-ending civil war from 1975 to 1990, resulting in an estimated 150,000 deaths and the exodus of almost one million people from the country. More recently in 2020, Beirut was rocked by the massive explosion of unprotected silos of ammonium nitrate. The blast devastated swaths of the city and the harbour, severely damaging the country's economy, destabilising its delicately-balanced political system, and leaving over 300,000 people homeless.

Arriving in Beirut, we expected to find a partially devastated and possibly dangerous city in a country hampered by a non-functioning government. What we found was different – on the surface at least. There had been no tourists since October 2023 but life still appeared normal. Beirut, the international business hub for the region, seemed unaffected. We noticed cranes everywhere and property prices were booming. The beaches were full, the shopping centres were all open with decorative stores selling international brands and cash machines dispensing US dollars only. In fact, the only currency widely in use and accepted was cash, preferably US dollars. Anyone with a car, can offer visitors a taxi service for cash and many do, even if they are not officially registered as taxis. Prices for the same distance can vary from $5 – $20. Our first experience after landing at the airport and clearing immigration with no arrival fees, was being overcharged for the taxi from the airport to the city – $45 vs $20 for the same return journey ten days later. It happened everywhere.

Across the streets from where we stayed in the Radisson Hotel Verdun, there was the ABC shopping Centre, a large, chic mall, right in the city centre. The endless seafront was stunning, lined with dramatic high rise apartment buildings all with underground parking, security and elaborate extras. But the footpaths and public services are terrible. Despite nearly being a failed state, Lebanon still manages to function for those with means, while the struggles of the less fortunate remain largely invisible to visitors. Exclusively on the Mediterranean, the city location has everything – the famous seafront, Corniche and, just an hour away, skiing on Mt. Lebanon, and to the west lies the island of Cyprus.

Beirut seafront

The Raouché (aka Pigeon's Rock)

The following morning, both of us were up early for a walk on the Corniche. We shared a Turkish coffee in the ocean-side café with the sea lapping the coast while nearby teenagers were diving and swimming from the rocky shore.

Onwards to the Beirut Museum, which was a highlight (and I am not a great museum visitor, my son, on the other hand, soaks up all these details). The displays were from all the Ages, from prehistory to today. Our lasting memory was the dedication to Emir Maurice Chehab (1904 – 1994).

Emir Maurice Chehab, after whom the gallery is named, was the first Lebanese Director of Antiquities. He dedicated his life to archaeology, to the protection of cultural heritage and also to the rescue of the national antiquities. From 1928, he contributed to the creation of the Beirut National Museum and became the Chief of Antiquities in 1944, eventually becoming General Director in 1960. He was a highly distinguished archaeologist and undertook excavations on the Lebanese territory for over forty years, more specifically in Tyre.

During the Lebanese civil war (1975 – 1991), Chehab succeeded in saving the Beirut National Museum's archaeological collections by building concrete blocks and masonry walls, behind which the objects were safely preserved. During the 1992 civil war he saved the building and its contents from being ravaged and destroyed. The museum was located on the aptly named Green Line which divided the city and its warring factions. *(Can you imagine having the National Museum of Ireland placed on the Peace Line in Belfast during the Troubles?)*

For lunch close by, we found Kudeta Bistro – *il Gusto* is run by a charming and charismatic Lebanese owner. We enjoyed it so much that we returned two nights later for their lively karaoke night. The place was packed, with diners belting out nostalgic French classics in true

Édith Piaf style. The French influence and sense of nostalgia here are unmistakable and created a memorable atmosphere.

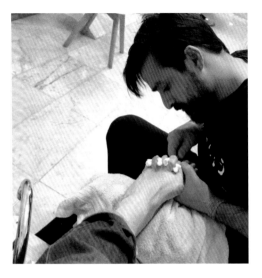

On the first day here, I developed a very sore corn on my left foot. At my age, closer to 80 than to 75, I considered it a high priority to get my feet in good shape before starting on our 22-day trek. With some sign language and Google, I explained my dilemma to the front desk manager who made an appointment for me for 11am the following morning at Nadar Salon for Gentleman. I travelled by taxi, 10 kms into the heart of the southern area of Beirut. Lots of army and police checks were here, maybe because this is also the main route south. It is, as we later discovered, a Hezbollah stronghold – an area not to be recommended and since then, subjected to Israeli bombardment. My driver refused to leave me and finally, we found the Nadar Gentlemen's Lab, a beauty, cosmetic and personal care salon for men. Nader had recently returned from training and working in the Netherlands and he opened an hour early, especially for me. When he heard where I was from, he turned on his music and out blared *The Fields of Athenry*. When it came to paying, he refused the full amount and would only take $12. The taxi driver looked on in disbelief. I later thanked him by text and he responded with, 'you're most welcome Habibi – it's your place!' I returned to our hotel minus a corn and like a dancer after a foot massage.

The following morning, Denis went for a run and a swim on the nearby beach and I, with my new foot, walked along the Corniche, just two blocks from our hotel. The sun was shining, the sea sparkling and I felt excited and optimistic about our travel plans. After an hour, I found myself near a complex called *Dream Bay* and decided it was time to turn back. Trusting in my own flawless sense of direction, I was certain I wouldn't get lost with the sea as my guide.

But I did.

Having circled the same block twice, I finally acknowledged I was undeniably lost. I asked a parked taxi driver how far it was to my hotel. 'Ten minutes,' he said but I didn't believe him. At that very moment, a man wearing a red jacket and helmet was leaving his nearby apartment with his motorbike and, observing my predicament, said, 'Hop on.' And I did!

Riding a pillion with one arm around him and my hiking pole in the other, he brought me back to the hotel. Mohammed, my saviour, was an ex-Lebanon army officer who now worked as head of security for an insurance company. Waving him off, I recorded the episode on my phone. I was hysterical with laughter for a full five minutes, probably out of relief. Any anxiety I had about our trip, evaporated in that motor bike trip.

Denis had a different experience and met up with a younger local group on the beach who were dancing to a boom box, pumping out music while taking selfies.

The second evening, after dinner in a downtown area across from the harbour in a quirky rebuilt Temple Bar type area, we took a taxi back to the hotel. I had only just arrived in our bedroom when, checking my pocket, I had the horrible realisation that I had no phone. Losing my phone in this context was, for me, catastrophic. It is not just an extension of my limbs and mind – it's an integral part of who I am. Also, all our information, our contacts and instructions, were on it. Trying to retrace our steps, I tried to remember if we had taken a photo of the taxi or taken the driver's name. We had done neither. The usual panic questions arose... What did he look like? Maybe it was she? What colour or make was the car? Was there anything that we could identify or trace to find the taxi. Did it have a taxi sign? Probably not as practically everyone with a car in Beirut moonlighted as a taxi driver – this was my living nightmare.

Trying to appear as a responsible adult, with my head thumping, I took the lift down four floors to the reception and blurted out the story. Of course we will offer a large reward, I said. Should we call the police? Is there a taxi authority? Deep down I believed that the questions were futile.

Still in panic mode we raced out through the glass doors, down the six marble steps, to the Radisson Hotel front entrance with security guards, screening machines for incoming guests and uniformed porters. We told our story. We got nothing but a sympathetic look, if they understood at all.

Back in the coffee shop in the lobby, I couldn't speak. Unbelievably, within 20 minutes the man from the front desk approached us with a big smile saying, 'The taxi is outside with your phone – you should go.' I practically ran out and yes, there was the driver with my bright red iPhone. A true traveller's miracle – Annie's Travel Angel and prayers to Our Lady of Lebanon had worked their wonders. A grateful decent dollar tip, handshakes and hugs and calm returned. I felt I might need a drink; the hotel didn't have a bar and the coffee shop only served wine. It sufficed. We were back on track.

Next day, we travelled outside Beirut north and west. We visited the Jeita Grotto, with the longest underground river in the Middle East, where subterranean caves are world-renowned for their stalactites and stalagmites. Then onto the Maronite Shrine of Our Lady of Lebanon, and finally for the day, to the city of Byblos. Including the other three people on the tour, we were the only guests in a 100-seater restaurant overlooking the ancient harbour.

Jeita Grotto   *Our Lady of Lebanon*

Denis went for a swim. I walked back to the centre of Byblos, which is normally one of Lebanon's major visitor destinations. One main street, almost a kilometre in length, was lined with shops and stalls – all open, all empty. Even the unique fossil shop for locally mined ancient fossils was empty, except for us.

RR Le Royal Hotel

On the return trip to Beirut, one of the most memorable sights was that of the RR Le Royal, a vast, shuttered up resort hotel and complex. Our guide pointed it out to us saying: 'That's owned by Saddam Hussein's daughter.' I found it disturbingly eerie. Arriving back to our drop-off point, we took an old silver-grey Mercedes taxi to our hotel. The sixty-year-old driver asked where we were from. When we said we were from Ireland, he exclaimed with pleasure, 'Welcome Irish – me Hezbollah – you Sinn Fein.'

Never forgetting the wider context of where we were, I was in regular contact with Untamed Borders to check the status and safety issues around our journey plan. They verified with their people on the ground in Syria and reassured us that all was on schedule.

This is a sample of updates from them:

> *The attacks by Iran on Israel over the weekend do constitute an escalation in general in the region. It does, of course, increase the risk overall of a major conflict between Israel and Iran. Given that both the Syria and (part of the) Lebanon governments are Iranian allies, this does increase risk.*
>
> *However, it appears that it appears to be just a show of strength by Iran. Neither Syria nor Lebanon was involved. We do expect there to be some further retribution in the future by Israel but all elements in the region are seemingly working to reduce the chances of further escalation.*
>
> *Given this, there does not seem an imminent danger of indiscriminate bombing by Israel in Syria. As such we are still planning to run your trip.*
>
> *Note that we currently have one guest in Syria, and we plan to complete his tour this week.*
>
> *We are aware that the events may be very disconcerting and should you be concerned and wish to postpone the trip then please do let us know.*

Another email:

> *Please note your safety is paramount. We are constantly checking the news and other security reports and receiving updates from our team in Syria. Any further updates I will be in touch. The other two guests are still happy to join the trip so you will all meet at the starting hotel.*

We did feel reassured.

Denis's thoughts:

Morning adventures in Beirut

Our first morning, I went for a jog armed with my few words of Arabic and encountered a charming array of cats along the way. Some seemed to size me up before boldly stepping forward. I struck up conversations with a friendly taxi driver and a security guard carrying a gun, both of whom seemed genuinely pleased to see me – perhaps because there hadn't been many tourists in recent months. The roads posed a challenge, lined with oddly placed defensive walls and lacking clear crossings. Large posters of politicians adorned the streets, which were dusty and filled with hot air. It was evident that while the country had huge wealth, the coordination of public services left much to be desired.

Finally, I made my way to the promenade, which had clearly seen better days. The lifeguard huts were old and rusted and litter dotted the area. After a refreshing shower back at the hotel, Dad and I set out to explore downtown along the famous Corniche – which was in better condition than the other side I had visited earlier. My father has an uncanny ability to assess how a city functions; he pointed out details of evident wealth that I might have otherwise overlooked, like car dealerships and cranes. As we walked, I noticed men running with their tops off and a diverse mix of women's styles – some covered up in Muslim dress, others wearing more Western fashions – exuding glamour and confidence. The atmosphere was a curious blend of contrasts.

We then went to the National Museum of Beirut which holds a treasure trove of artefacts from one million-year-old flint cutting tools used by Homo Erectus up to stone age and bronze age jewellery and mummies and pottery and statues created by later civilisations. We were both fascinated and it felt our tour had truly begun.

On the beach in Beirut

An Unexpected Dance

That afternoon, I headed to the beach, where a group of guys blasted Arabic rap tunes. To my surprise, just ten metres away, a group of women danced along. Intrigued, I approached the men to ask who they were listening to. Although they didn't speak English, they understood my question and shared the names of the musicians on my Spotify. Soon, they were dancing, and I joined in. One of the men wore a Palestinian chain around his neck, and I made a prayer gesture, saying, 'Palestine, salaam inshallah (peace God-willing).' When they asked where I was from, I replied, 'Irlanda.' After a moment of confusion, one of them exclaimed, 'Ah, we love Ireland!' and embraced me.

We danced again to the music, sharing handshakes and man hugs before I headed back to grab my things. A pair of young men in their mid-twenties asked my name and where I was from. One asked for my number, hoping I could help him get a visa. I gave him my Instagram handle and mumbled that I'd do what I could.

Later, Dad and I ventured out to grab a bite to eat. The quality of the bars and restaurants was striking – many of them built since the terrible port explosion in 2020 – this city was truly a phoenix, which made sense as the name 'phoenix' is derived from Greek 'φοῖνιξ' (phoenix), meaning 'dark red' and etymologists believe the name shares roots with the ancient people of the Mediterranean called the Phoenicians (from modern day Lebanon), who were known for making a coveted purple-red dye extracted from the murex shellfish (Tyrian Purple).

As we walked to find a restaurant I kept spotting buildings and sights that seemed phenomenal, my mind so alive in this place, and I excitedly pointed them out to Dad, who sensibly remained steadfastly focused on navigating the uneven ground with his walking stick. One step at a time. A good approach to life!

Denis' thoughts on our tour:

Jeita Grotto was one of the most spectacular natural wonders I had ever seen. There were only a couple of other tourists where usually there would be hundreds. The scale of the caverns and stalactites and stalagmites was like something from a fantastical movie, and then we visited a second Grotto where we took a boat for hundreds of metres on crystal blue waters underground. I kept saying WOW and I meant it! Our guide Albert was funny and knowledgeable, and our three tour companions were from Cyprus and England and were really interesting to chat with. It was a super day.

Next we visited the gorgeous Maronite Church complex surrounded by cedar trees on the hills overlooking Beirut dedicated to Our Lady (The Maronites derive their name from Saint Maron, a Syriac Christian whose followers migrated to the area of Mount Lebanon from their previous place of residence around the area of Antioch and established the nucleus of the Maronite Church which today has approximately 10 million followers).

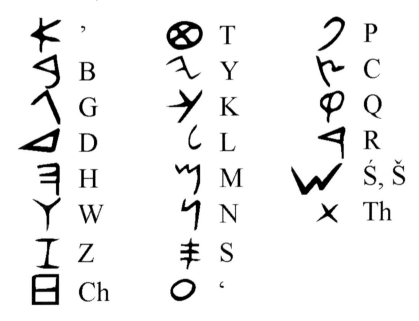

The Phoenician Alphabet: Phoenician alphabet – Definition, Letters, & History
© Britannica' www.britannica.com.

And then we made our way to Byblos, one of the oldest and cities in the world:

We read the area is believed to have been first settled between 8800
and 7000 BC and continuously inhabited since 5000 BC. During its

history, Byblos was part of numerous cultures including Egyptian, Phoenician, Assyrian, Persian, Hellenistic, Roman, Genoese, Mamluk and Ottoman. Urbanisation is thought to have begun during the third millennium BC and it developed into a city making it one of the oldest cities in the world. It is a UNESCO World Heritage Site. It was in Ancient Byblos that the Phoenician alphabet, likely the ancestor of the Greek, Latin and all other Western alphabets, was developed.

Garfinkel, Yosef (2004). 'Néolithique' et 'Énéolithique' Byblos in Southern Levantine Context. Oxbow Books.

Harbour at Byblos

The harbour in Byblos was small and perfectly formed. Dad and I stood there and imagined the Phoenician ships thousands of years before setting out across the Mediterranean to establish trading links between many diverse peoples and spread the technological wonder of their alphabet and sell their coveted purple dyes (Tyrian Purple) which became the colour of the robes of the Roman Emperors. Something that really made an impression on me in Byblos was seeing a family of traders packing up their table of souvenirs to prepare to go home at 4pm. We saw no other tourists while we were in Byblos that day. Perhaps there had been a handful of others. The traders knew they would sell almost nothing, and yet they had packed up their cars, set up their stalls with their children, and showed up for their day's work with dignity.

On the (often-nerve-wracking!) drive back to Beirut Albert drove past the port where the tragic explosion had occurred in 2020:

On 4 August 2020, a large amount of ammonium nitrate stored at the Port of Beirut in the capital city of Lebanon exploded, causing at least 218 deaths, 7,000 injuries, and US$15 billion in property damage, as well as leaving an estimated 300,000 people homeless. A cargo of 2,750 tonnes of the substance (equivalent to around 1.1 kilotons of TNT) had been stored in a warehouse without proper safety measures for the previous six years after having been confiscated by Lebanese authorities from the abandoned ship MV Rhosus. A fire in the same warehouse preceded the explosion. The blast was so powerful that it was felt throughout Lebanon. It was also felt in Turkey, Syria, Palestine, Jordan, Israel, and parts of Europe, and was heard in Cyprus, more than 240 km (150 mi) away. It was detected by the United States Geological Survey as a seismic event of magnitude 3.3 and is considered one of the biggest ever non-nuclear explosions.

McRae, Mike (19 March 2021). 'The Tragic Beirut Explosion Was So Violent, It Disturbed Earth's Ionosphere'. ScienceAlert.

Albert pointed out a stunning 25-metre sculpture made by Nadim Karam of a person holding a dove made from debris from the blast.

The work was put together over nine months using the scrap metal of wrecked hangars retrieved from the port area. The project was implemented with the support of a community of professionals who contributed materials, manpower or expertise; it intends to offer a gesture of solidarity and hope to the city.

www.nadimkaram.com

Exploring Baalbek

The next day, I left Dad behind to go on a day trip to Anjar and Baalbek. Our driver Hassane, and the other passenger Hussein – who was visiting from Houston, were both Shia Muslims. They were both chatty and told me they were deeply concerned about the ongoing violence in Gaza. Hussein shared his recent experiences in Jerusalem and at the Al Aqsa Mosque, the second holiest site in Islam, where he faced a rough six-hour interrogation at the airport. Hassane expressed his sadness, saying he'd likely never be able to visit Al Aqsa himself because of his nationality. They both showed me videos purporting to be of Israeli teenagers on a video-call with a Palestinian man telling him they hoped he died of cancer. Was this real, was this fake? I had no idea. But it made them even angrier about people who they saw as the enemy.

With Hassane & Hussein

As we arrived in Anjar, we enjoyed a guided tour of the first Muslim city, which was built at the beginning of the 8th century and in just ten years by slaves under Umayyad caliph al-Walid I. We were again the only tourists at this historic site and our guide, an Armenian, informed us that Armenians had founded Anjar after fleeing the genocide in World War I.

Umayyad city at Anjar

The Marvels of Baalbek

Upon reaching Baalbek, sellers of head-coverings (keffiyehs) and fake Roman coins asked us to buy their wares. We haggled a bit and I bought both. Again, we found ourselves alone among the ruins. For an archaeology enthusiast, this place was a dream come true. The impressive structures were built with the trading wealth of the Phoenicians and later reconstructed by the Romans. Our guide showed us colossal stones, some weighing up to 50 tons and the majestic columns that still stood tall.

The Archaeologist at Baalbek

We entered the Temple of Dionysus (Denis in Greek) where we paused to listen to the history and marvel at the magnificent surroundings. Our guide, one of Lebanon's top archaeologists, proudly shared that his grandfather had been the first guide in the country, with his father following in his footsteps. He lamented the erosion of discipline in the modern world but praised the Germans for their archaeological contributions – all delivered with a warm, knowing smile.

With Hussein in support of Palestine

As we drove back through Baalbek, the contrast with cosmopolitan Beirut was striking. Posters on every lamppost of dead Hezbollah militants and the ultra-conservative attire of both men and women created a different atmosphere. Baalbek had been influenced and infiltrated by Iranian military and religious agents in the 1980s, leading to a more repressive environment and drawing young men into the orbit of militant Islam.

Hezbollah leaders

At the time of writing Baalbek is in the news once again as Israel targets Hezbollah:

> *Israel – air strikes on Lebanon kill 40 people around Baalbek'. Reuters 7th November 2024.*

> *When cross-border hostilities broke out between Israel and Hezbollah in southern Lebanon more than a year ago, Baalbek and the wider Bekaa Valley were largely spared. But in recent weeks, Israel has*

increasingly turned its sights eastward, laying waste to the fertile yet impoverished region known for its agriculture, vineyards and Roman temples.

Hezbollah was founded here 40 years ago, and draws support from the Shia-majority communities that populate its plains and depend on its patronage. The Bekaa's proximity to the Syrian border has made it a strategic corridor through which weapons, contraband and military personnel flow between Lebanon and Hizbollah's allies in Syria, Iraq and Iran.

Financial Times 19 November 2024

A Visit to the Mosque

Mosque in Baalbek

Bullet outside Mosque   *Tomb of Sayyida Khawla*

Our next stop was a stunning mosque we had passed on the outskirts of Baalbek. Before entering I put on tracksuit bottoms to cover my legs. Inside, I found a two-foot-tall bullet standing next to a recruitment poster, with mosaics of Islamic martyrs decorating the walls. Men gathered in the courtyard, surrounded by exquisite Iranian decorations adorned with Quranic verses in stunning blue, white and navy hues.

Surprisingly, the men spoke openly inside the mosque. Hassane encouraged me to take photos and Hussein even FaceTimed his parents to share this significant place of worship for Shia Muslims (it houses the tomb of Sayyida Khawla, the daughter of Imam Hussein and great granddaughter of Prophet Muhammad). Hassane showed me how they prayed, and we took a few moments to pray for peace in Palestine – up, down, him reciting verses from the Quran, me responding Allahu akbar. I could understand how Muslims fall into a trance-like state while praying. I felt honoured to share that moment with Hassane.

We chatted about various topics – The Prophet and his companions, their journey from Mecca to Medina, the Hajj and even the differences between Christianity and Islam. Hassane mentioned, in his view, the potential danger of up to 50,000 ISIS fighters hiding in Syrian refugee camps in Lebanon, a ticking time bomb he said. I wondered if that number could possibly be true or if it was misinformation.

When the conversation turned to Ayatollah Khamenei and his predecessor Ayatollah Khomeini, I asked Hassane about the brutal repression following Khomeini's rise to power in 1979, and the recent attacks on women. He seemed to praise the regime without harsh criticism – and he didn't seem to be aware of or want to acknowledge the recent viciousness. I debated a bit with him but there was no point arguing so I just listened and tried to understand his views about marriage and religion and history. It was hugely interesting to understand the world through his and Hussein's eyes. They saw so much of the West as being decadent and sinful (or perhaps had absorbed these opinions from Imams). And yet Hassane also admitted he liked a drink and said though he tried his best he was not as good a Muslim as he should be. He had strong opinions but was also aware of his own flaws.

Wine Tasting at Château Ksara

Before heading back, we made a stop at Château Ksara, Lebanon's oldest winery. Surprisingly, Lebanon has a substantial wine industry, producing nearly 10 million bottles annually, half of which are exported. The winery's history dates back to 1857 when Jesuit monks acquired the property, applying their expertise in science and agriculture to cultivate French vines and create Roman caves for wine storage. Château Ksara produces about three million bottles a year, exporting to over 40 countries. www.chateauksara.com

After a brief tour and delicious tasting, we returned to the car, and we sped through the Bekaa Valley back toward Beirut. As we arrived at the hotel, we exchanged goodbyes, each of us carrying the day's memories with us.

IRELAND AND LEBANON

The bond of peacekeeping – 47 Irish soldiers have given up their lives in this mission.

Ireland and Lebanon have a long connection, forged during my own lifetime, (we actually met one Irish peacekeeper during our brief visit – a very friendly guy who we met on the street in Damascus as we both looked at each other and recognised our mutual Irishness!). Ireland has a long-standing history of peacekeeping in the country, primarily through its involvement with the United Nations Interim Force in Lebanon (UNIFIL). Irish peacekeepers first arrived in the country in 1958 as part of a UN Observer Group, marking the beginning of Ireland's continuous participation in UN peacekeeping missions worldwide. In the Middle East, Irish UN peacekeepers and observers have served in the the Israeli-occupied Syrian Golan Heights (seized by Israel at the end of the 1967 Six Day war, and since then annexed by it but still officially part of Syria) in Syria proper, in Israel itself and in Jordan, as well as in many other parts of the world.

UNIFIL was set up in 1978, following a Lebanon-based Palestinian attack on Israel and subsequent Israeli invasion of Lebanon. UNIFIL's role was to patrol a buffer zone in southern Lebanon, between the border with Israel and north to the Litani River in Lebanon, observing the ceasefire agreement, ensuring the zone was demilitarised and assisting the Lebanon government maintain authority in the zone. Israel has long criticised the UN for, as they see it, the ineffectiveness of the UNIFIL mission. Ireland contributes a full contingent of 650 soldiers to this mission. Over the years, Irish troops have been involved in various peacekeeping activities, including providing humanitarian assistance and patrolling conflict zones. The Irish Defence Forces have faced significant challenges, including attacks from militant groups and tragic incidents resulting in casualties. To date, 47 Irish soldiers have died while serving with UNIFIL. But despite these dangers, Irish troops continue their mission, currently serving alongside Polish peacekeepers and conducting joint patrols with Lebanese forces. Ireland's commitment to peacekeeping reflects its values of neutrality and international cooperation, contributing significantly to stability in the region

The Irish Defence Forces have maintained a focus on traditional peacekeeping, working alongside Lebanese national forces to conduct joint patrols and provide humanitarian support. Despite the challenges, including the loss of 47 Irish soldiers over the years, Ireland continues to play a crucial role in maintaining stability in the region. As I write, UNIFIL peacekeepers in southern Lebanon are in danger of getting caught in crossfire between Israel and Hezbollah, or worse, coming under direct fire from either side, which has happened thankfully to date, with no casualties.

Author's Note (Denis): *Since our visit to Lebanon, Israel stepped up its attacks on Hezbollah, including killing 42 people and injuring 3,500 via exploding pagers and walkie-talkies in an incident that was dubbed Operation Grim Beeper. While Israel's attacks on Hezbollah targets in Beirut displaced 1.2m people and killed hundreds of civilians as well as killing many militants, a ceasefire has since been agreed, brokered by the Biden administration. At the time of writing, it seems that these events have the potential to weaken Hezbollah's grip on Lebanon (as well as eroding their influence in Syria) which has impeded progress in the country for decades. Time will tell.*

While Lebanon faces many challenges, and has suffered so many horrendous difficulties in the recent past, it is also an incredibly vibrant & modern place which we loved visiting. And with 18 different religious denominations living there, the country is, for the most part, a rare miracle of co-existence & tolerance that is worth understanding and celebrating.

Old: Temple of Bacchus/Dionysus (Baalbek)

New: The ABC Mall in Beirut

SYRIA

Syrian Arab Republic

(Arabic) ٱلْجُمْهُوْرِيَّةُ ٱلْعَرَبِيَّةُ ٱلسُّوْرِيَّةُ

al-Jumhūriyya al-ʿArabiyya as-Sūriyya

Author's Note: *As we publish this account, in Syria, rebels sweep through the country from the north, taking Damascus in a matter of days as Assad and his family flee the country for Russia. A reminder that this is a region where nothing changes and then suddenly, everything changes.*

We said our goodbyes to Beirut and hit the road. Our departure on the morning of April 20th was set for 8 AM from a pickup point in the heart of downtown, within the business district's sleek towers. A short taxi ride brought us to our meeting spot, where Ibraheem, our security driver, greeted us. He would be guiding us to the Syrian border in a sleek, cream-coloured, 6-seater business class van, equipped with armrests and handy compartments for water and phones – a nice touch of comfort for the road ahead. Beirut to Damascus is just a short 110 kms road journey.

We were pleasantly surprised to find we weren't travelling alone. Joining us were two fellow adventurers, Erin and Francesca. Erin, hailing from Detroit, living in Oman for the past five years as a university lecturer and food travel blogger. Her extensive travels through the region were evident in her stories and enthusiasm. Francesca, on the other hand, a logistics project manager in London, focusing on major transport infrastructure projects. (Francesca joined us with a very recent basketball injury – a black eye.) A Canadian with Romanian roots, her passion for the region began when she wrote her master's thesis on the environmental impact of Syria's civil war. Both women were travelling solo and had only just met, we clicked instantly, setting the tone for the adventure ahead.

Denis's thoughts:

Before we left Lebanon we stopped off at a money exchange where we each changed US$100 into Syrian pounds which was worth 1,400,000SYP. We needed plastic bags to hold our bricks of cash. We all shared a laugh as it was absurd to us as tourists, but it was also sad as it spoke volumes of the daily reality for people struggling to survive in a country of runaway inflation.

Arrival in Syria

We entered the Syrian Arab Republic, its official name, at the Al Jdeideh Crossing, where we were met by Mr. Taysir, our guide for the next seven days. He greeted us with a smile, showing his official Ministry of Tourism card – complete with photograph, stamps and dates – before swiftly taking charge. He handled everything with ease, from our entry permits to negotiating the entry fees, the amounts depending, without obvious reason, on from which country the person came: $75 each for the Irish, $100 for Francesca and $200 for Erin. Looming above us in the hot sunshine was a life-sized image of President Bashar Al Assad, a presence that would soon become a familiar sight throughout our journey in Syria.

Mr. Taysir's English was impeccable as he explained that we'd head straight to Damascus, about half an hour away, where another driver would meet us before continuing our trip. As we descended the hills that separate Lebanon from Syria, the suburbs of Damascus came into view. Our first stop was near a public park, where the local manager from Untamed Borders greeted us.

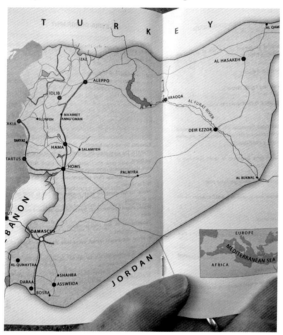

He handed out our itineraries, neatly bound in small, understated black-and-white booklets. The details were intentionally sparse, a precaution for security reasons. We had been briefed earlier not to share too much about our trip, especially avoiding conversations about our accommodations or reasons for visiting Syria. The operator made it clear that plans could change depending on circumstances, which added a layer of unpredictability – but also a sense of safety.

Our sleek van was then swapped for an older, more discreet model, and we met our new driver, Jusuf. A quiet, serious man with a background in the army, Jusuf took his role as driver and guardian with great attentiveness. Both he and Taysir, like many Syrians we would meet, were heavy smokers and soon enough, we settled into our routine. Each of us naturally fell into our usual seats in the van: Jusuf behind the wheel with Taysir beside him; I sat directly behind Taysir and Denis behind Jusuf; Erin took her spot behind Denis and Francesca next to her. We had our supplies of water, nuts and sweets in the back while the front was stocked with cigarettes for the crew. In a short time, we had become a well-organised team, six people with a shared purpose.

On the road into Syria

As we drove, I reflected on Syria's layered history. After the fall of the Ottoman Empire following World War I, Syria was governed by France until it gained independence in 1946. The CIA facts book mentions that Syrians are among the lightest drinkers in the world, averaging just 0.13 litres of alcohol per year. According to the History Channel, Syria is also part of the Fertile Crescent, often called the Cradle of Civilization. This fertile region spans parts of modern-day Egypt, Jordan, Israel, Palestine, Syria, Turkey, Iran, Iraq and Cyprus – an ancient and storied land, rich in history, now awaiting our exploration.

Denis's thoughts on entering Syria:

Author's Note: *As this book is being completed for printing in December 2024, we have been watching the events in Syria with amazement as the Assad regime has fallen. As more and more information emerges, the endless evils perpetrated by the tyrant (and before him his father Hafez) and his enablers are becoming clear. It also turns out that Assad kept his government afloat funded by $10bn in annual sales of the illicit drug Captagon which was manufactured around the country. While there is great uncertainty about the future, it seems to me that the fall of this hideous regime is very much something worth celebrating, as is the outpouring of joy & emotion from Syrians in Damascus and around the world. There may be difficulties ahead as Syrians attempt to chart a path forwards, and it may not be a smooth road towards the establishment of a unified democratic state which treats women equally and which respects all ethnicities & faiths, but with luck & time I am hopeful that this wonderful country can find its feet. And that its wonderful people can finally enjoy the hope & opportunities they deserve, which for so long they were denied. With luck this will turn out to have been the liberation of Syria & Syrians. (In sha' Allah / God-willing.)*

You know very quickly after crossing the border that you are in Syria. And that Syria is ruled by a thin man with a discreet moustache. As you drive further into the country you will see enormous images of him on buildings, billboards and a variety of other installations. In some of these he is holding babies, in others he is visiting the sick in hospital, and in others he is wearing aviator shades while donning a military uniform looking like he has walked off the set for Top Gun 3. In yet others he is pictured smiling with his wife Asma. You could be forgiven for thinking this was a great man, a doer of great deeds. This, however, is the cult of strong-man propaganda, mindwashing at scale. The ubiquity of his image reveals more about his insecurity than it does his power.

This man's name is Bashar al-Assad, and he has been accused of a multitude of war crimes:

> *'French investigative judges have issued an international arrest warrant for President Bashar al-Assad of Syria that accuses him of complicity in war crimes and crimes against humanity over the deadly use of chemical weapons against his own people, a judicial official said on Wednesday.'*
> New York Times 15/11/23

A few hours after entering the country our irrepressible guide Taysir tells me that he and Yusuf the driver believe that I bear an uncanny resemblance to their

President al-Assad. My Dad, Erin and Fran burst out laughing. Taysir says that as we are passing the frequent military checkpoints (which help maintain an uneasy peace across Syria which does not have many major roads) the soldiers are peering in our windows to see their President for themselves. This is not a resemblance one would choose! But I have to admit it's kind of funny... and I laugh along with the others... through gritted teeth :)

Our new van was comfortable, though noticeably older – a choice, I suspect, to blend in more easily. It seemed like an unassuming vehicle would attract less attention here. We headed northwest along nearly empty highways, with Jusuf driving fast and attentive. The road signs we zipped past were surreal – one pointing towards Jordan, another towards Iran and a third towards Iraq. In the vast, almost barren landscape, it all felt like some strange mirage.

By early afternoon, hunger set in, but we were still on the move. Finally, Jusuf pulled into a roadside service area. The first thing we saw was a weathered sign that could have come straight out of a Wild West movie, featuring an image of Assad alongside a recently assassinated Iranian leader, both holding AK-47s. It was a jarring backdrop as we disembarked, eager for a break.

The service area was a mix of stalls selling nuts, sweets and ice cream, alongside a large barn-like building that housed a self-service café with restrooms. The café's specialty was a mini pizza, just the right size for one person, topped generously with pesto. It was a welcome, if unexpected, meal. We peeled off wads of the local currency – bundles that felt like bricks in our pockets – to pay, though the total for everything probably came to less than $2.

Before we re-boarded, Denis couldn't resist stopping by the nuts stall, a true emporium with hundreds of varieties and a roasting machine hard at work. Syria, it turns out, is a major grower of nuts and we left with a stash to fuel the rest of our journey.

Krak

Back in the van, we began climbing into the foothills, passing through small villages until we finally arrived at the entrance of one of the most remarkable and well-preserved Crusader castles still standing today – Krak des Chevaliers. The journey from Damascus, including a short break, took over two hours. Even T. E. Lawrence, famously known as Lawrence of Arabia, once described Krak des Chevaliers as 'perhaps the best preserved and most wholly admirable castle in the world,' calling it a fitting testament to the Crusading architecture of Syria.

Before the civil war, Krak des Chevaliers attracted over half a million visitors annually, surrounded by bustling restaurants and hotels. Today, those once-thriving businesses are abandoned, their windows hollowed out, leaving behind a ghostly atmosphere. The castle itself sits perched on an unassailable hilltop, commanding breathtaking views over vast fertile valleys and scattered villages. Incredibly, we were the only visitors.

Exploring the castle felt like stepping into another world. It's a labyrinth of defensive structures – castles within castles, with soaring turrets, algae-coloured moats, luxury horse stables, chapels, kitchens, latrines, storerooms and secret passages. The sheer scale and complexity of the place were astonishing, like a defensive Rubik's cube designed to house thousands of Crusading soldiers, their horses and everything needed to withstand a siege or launch an attack. Krak des Chevaliers is truly a marvel of mediaeval military architecture and wandering through its vast, silent corridors, we couldn't help but feel the weight of history in every stone.

Taysir led us energetically through the castle, marching us up, down and around its impressive grounds. After years without tourists to guide, he was in his element – proudly storytelling at every turn. He even showed us his favourite selfie spot on the parapet of the Commander's Tower. We could pose as if we had heroically scaled the wall, our heads just peeking over the top, all thanks to a hidden ledge below.

Denis's Thoughts:

What a day, what a place – from desert plains to lush valleys! And the Krak was truly mighty! The most impressive castle I had ever seen (until the equally impressive Saladin Castle a few days later in Aleppo!). Fran and Erin were wonderful travel companions and could find humour in almost any situation. On our first stop at the petrol station we had stocked up on every kind of snack we could find – crisps and cakes and nuts and bananas and some sweet treats we had never seen before. Snackfest. There were frequent military checkpoints and many armed army officers – almost all of whom smiled and waved when we waved and said hi from the van. Taysir was the perfect guide – with 40 years of experience and full of fun and insight. After all the anxiety and uncertainty in advance of our trip, it was wonderful to finally be in Syria.

Later, we enjoyed our first dinner together at a nearby guesthouse called Beibars, where the owner himself cooked and served a delicious meal. As night descended, Jusuf navigated us to the Al Wadi Hotel, located some distance away. The drive through the villages felt eerie, with nightly power rationing leaving most streets in near-total darkness. Only the occasional streetlight flickered as we passed.

Before reaching the hotel, we made a quick stop at a small grocery store opposite. 'Tomorrow is a long day. Not many places to get food. Buy what you need now,' Taysir urged us. The selection was limited, but we stocked up on essentials – nuts, biscuits, crisps and water.

At the hotel, the manager and six staff members welcomed us warmly with fruit drinks. The hotel's 1970s décor greeted us in the form of dark furniture and dim lighting, but by that point, we were simply grateful to have arrived. Exhausted, we settled in for the night.

The next morning, we gathered for breakfast – fresh local bread with hummus and of course, more nuts. The hotel was quiet, with only two other guests from the region. We were alone in this retro oasis, ready for the next chapter of our journey.

Palmyra

With breakfast behind us, we piled back into the van and set off for Palmyra, prepared for the long journey ahead through the desert. Armed with the supplies we had bought the evening before; we settled in for the hours of driving that lay ahead. The sun beat down, with temperatures climbing into the mid to high 30s as we drove east through the vast expanse of the Syrian Desert – a barren scrubland punctuated by patches of roadside tillage and the occasional line of windbreak trees. As we travelled, we saw herds of sheep and goats, tended by shepherds, grazing on the narrow strips of grass along the highway. There were no sizable towns, just a few scattered Bedouin-style canvas encampments dotting the landscape.

Roadside shop

Fran & Erin

Rice & petrol

Along stretches of the road, makeshift stalls appeared, selling essentials like water, petrol and diesel – often stored in transparent jerry cans – alongside bags of rice and nuts. It was a surprising contrast, the jerry cans of fuel lined up next to food staples in such a remote place. The stalls were a reminder of the resourcefulness of people living in the poorer regions of the world. Facilities were sparse. While we occasionally found temporary toilets, more often than not, it was a choice between wide open desert or basic squat toilets. And it was hot – relentlessly so. Jusuf, whenever possible, would stop at places he was familiar with, but we rarely came across regular petrol stations outside the larger cities.

At one stop, we watched a young man in charge of fuel sales, sitting cross-legged on the counter with two of his friends, leisurely smoking from a water pipe. It was a scene that felt timeless, offering a small glimpse into the rhythm of life in this remote part of Syria.

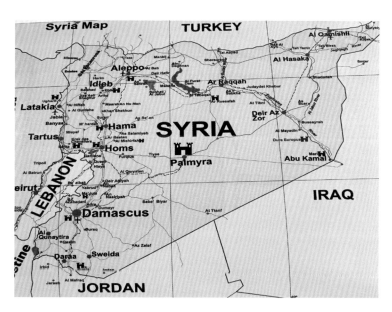

We arrived in the town of Palmyra just after midday, under a scorching sun. This once thriving town of over 50,000 residents had been reduced to rubble in May 2015, bombed by ISIS/Daesh. (The Islamic State, abbreviated IS, is also known as the Islamic State of Iraq and the Levant (ISIL /ˈaɪsɪl), the Islamic State of Iraq and Syria (ISIS /ˈaɪsɪs/), and by its Arabic acronym Da'ish or Daesh. Today, only about 10,000 people remain. Large parts of eastern Syria and Iraq had fallen under the control of ISIS, which declared it the Islamic State, a territory spanning nearly 100,000 square kilometres – larger than the entire island of Ireland.

Bullets from recent battles

There's a saying in Ireland about mad neighbours going out in the midday sun. Well, and on that day, we were certainly those people in Palmyra. After arriving and checking in with a local supervisor, our papers were reviewed and we were allowed to visit the ancient site, once known as the Venice of the Sands. Words fail to capture the grandeur this place must have held. Now, it's a scene of devastation. A few massive columns remain standing, like the remnants of a mouth missing most of its teeth. What had once been one of the wonders of the world now lies scattered, with enormous stones strewn haphazardly across hundreds of hectares, baking under the blazing sun.

With Taysir as our guide, we could still make out the layout of the place: the temple, the colosseum, the arena, the animal pens, the slave quarters and the ancient irrigation systems. But the sight of such destruction weighed heavily on me. This was, without a doubt, the most distressing day of our journey.

Taysir guiding us at Palmyra

To help us imagine what Palmyra once was, Taysir held up faded, sun-bleached postcards, contrasting the grandeur of the past with the missing teeth of the present. As the intense heat started to overwhelm me, I sought shade near a building at the edge of the site. Just as I was about to sit down on a rock, I heard a sharp, urgent shout: 'No! No! Not there! There could still be mines. Not all areas have been cleared yet.' I quickly moved back into the searing sun, shaken by the close call.

Taysir, ever the optimist, said, 'Yes, it's destroyed, but it will be rebuilt. The stones are still here. Archaeologists will eventually restore it.' Silently, I thought, perhaps, but not in our lifetime, Taysir. I later read that before 2011, Palmyra attracted up to one million visitors annually. Today, fewer than 5,000 make the journey. We saw no other visitors that day.

As we were leaving the ancient site, a small group of men, including the one who had granted us entry, had set up their meagre wares on a rock – old postcards, tattered guidebooks from before the war and a few beads and trinkets. After spending hours under the relentless sun and absorbing more history than I could manage, I retreated to the van. Jusuf, sensing my fatigue, kindly moved it into the shade beneath some standing columns and switched on the air conditioning, modest as it was. We exchanged a quiet glance, acknowledging the sadness of the scene and my exhaustion. With a cigarette in hand, he kept a distant but protective watch as Taysir led the others to explore another part of the site.

Out of the corner of my eye, I noticed a young boy, maybe six or seven, cautiously watching me from behind a rock. He stayed at a distance, nervously kicking a small stone. Slowly, as if trying to stay out of Jusuf's sight, he edged closer. When his friend joined him, they darted over to me in seconds, silently offering beads and rocks for sale. It was a wordless transaction – commerce in its simplest form. Then, suddenly, Jusuf appeared, and just as quickly as the boys had arrived, an older man followed, apologising and shooing them away. I felt a pang of sadness for the boys and their future in this shattered town. In another era, they might have been the merchants, guides or hotel owners of Palmyra, but conflict had stolen those dreams.

The abandoned museum at Palmyra

We returned to the town, where Taysir arranged a special visit to the once-celebrated museum of Palmyra. It was a shell of its former self, having been thoroughly pillaged. Only the stone carvings, too heavy to transport, remained.

> *At least 36 people have been killed and 50 wounded in an Israeli attack that hit residential buildings in the Syrian city of Palmyra, Syrian state media report. The air attack was launched from the direction of al-Tanf in eastern Syria and caused 'significant material damage', Syria's Ministry of Defence said in a statement on Wednesday that was quoted by the state news agency SANA. Al-Tanf is an area near the Iraqi border controlled by the United States.*
>
> 21 November 2024: Reuters and Aljazeera

Denis's thoughts:

This huge city in the desert must once have been some sight to behold. It was founded in the 3rd century BC at the crossroads of the trade routes which linked Europe and the Levant with the Silk Road. To be the only visitors was both special and sad. Taysir brought the ruins to life as he told us how the colonnades used to hold dozens of shops and baths. We heard about the enlightened Queen Zenobia who had rebelled against the Romans. We wandered around the magnificent ruins of the enormous old temple complex where one huge wall stood proudly, and then climbed up to a viewing platform where we could see for miles. We found bullets used in the battle between the Syrian army and ISIL in 2015. A father carrying his infant daughter beseeched us to buy his goods. I bought a faded guide book from 30 years ago. In normal times past this place would have been heaving with tourists from all over the world.

A Bedouin merchant and his daughter

Walking through the abandoned museum where fighting to the death had taken place just years before was surreal. A few large artefacts remained – pottery and mosaics and tombs – but most had been looted or moved.

Palmyra was founded in the 3rd millennium BC. The city grew wealthy from trade caravans; the Palmyrene became renowned as merchants who established colonies along the Silk Road and operated throughout the Roman Empire. Palmyra's wealth enabled the construction of monumental projects, such as the Great Colonnade, the Temple of Bel, and the distinctive tower tombs. Ethnically, the Palmyrenes combined elements of Amorites, Arameans, and Arabs. Socially structured around kinship and clans, Palmyra's inhabitants spoke Palmyrene Aramaic, a variety of Western Middle Aramaic, while using Koine Greek for commercial and diplomatic purposes. The Hellenistic period of West Asia influenced the culture of Palmyra, which produced distinctive art and architecture that combined different Mediterranean traditions. The city's inhabitants worshipped local Semitic, Mesopotamian and Arab deities.

By the third century AD, Palmyra had become a prosperous regional centre. It reached the apex of its power in the 260s, when the Palmyrene King Odaenathus defeated the Sasanian emperor Shapur 1. The king was succeeded by Queen regent Zenobia, who rebelled against Rome and established the Palmyrene Empire. Zenobia was a cultured monarch and fostered an intellectual environment in her court, which was open to scholars and philosophers. She was tolerant toward her subjects and protected religious minorities. The empress maintained a stable administration, which governed a multicultural, multiethnic empire until she was defeated in 273 by Roman Emperor Aurelian who destroyed Palmyra (which was later rebuilt by Diocletian at a reduced size). Zenobia died after 274, and many tales have been recorded about her fate. Her rise and fall have inspired historians, artists and novelists, and she is a patriotic symbol in Syria. Palmyra converted to Christianity during the fourth century and to Islam in the centuries following the conquest by the 7ᵗʰ-century Rashidun Caliphate, after which the Palmyrene and Greek languages were replaced by Arabic.

Veyne, Paul; Fagan, Teresa Lavender (2017). Palmyra. University of Chicago Press.

Taysir was tireless, squeezing every moment out of the day. His deep knowledge of Syria's history and culture was impressive, and he never hesitated to answer our questions. A proud and professional guide, he seemed unfazed by the heat or the endless walking, often smoking as he talked. He made sure we logged at least 12,000 to 15,000 steps each day – steps that we all felt by the end of it. Jusuf, our quiet, serious driver, was a different story – more focused on keeping us safe and pushing speed limits while smoking between checkpoints. Together, they made a perfect team to lead us through Syria.

The informal petrol refill

The drive west from Palmyra to Hama was a long, quiet one, passing through a region dotted with oil refineries. At one point, Jusuf pulled off onto an overpass, after making a phone call. A motorbike soon appeared; its back loaded with containers of fuel. Without a word, the two men emptied the petrol into the van's tank, exchanged money and off we went again. It was like a mobile fuel delivery service, something we would encounter again later in the trip. We wondered if this fuel was syphoned from the nearby refineries or just an entrepreneurial solution to the lack of regular petrol stations in the region.

Throughout our journey in Syria, whether heading east or west, we noticed the absence of heavy traffic but encountered military checkpoints every 20 kilometres or so. By now, we had become used to the drill: Jusuf would slow down as we approached, reminding us, 'No photos, no photos.' The soldier on duty would inspect the van, check our papers and wave us through. Just a hundred metres further, the same routine would repeat with another armed soldier. The checkpoints were serious, tense places, with groups of soldiers, AK-47s slung over their shoulders, watching everything. With so little traffic, it must be a monotonous job.

Traditional beehive grain silos

As we continued north towards Aleppo and back to Homs and Damascus, the military presence intensified near the cities, but for stretches of about 50 to 60 miles in between, the checkpoints vanished. When I asked about this, I was told that the areas to the west of the highway were still dangerous and likely controlled by anti-government forces. The tension was palpable, a reminder of Syria's ongoing struggles.

Hama

Arriving in Hama after dark, our van pulled up to a small side door on a narrow, hilly street – an unassuming entrance to our hotel for the night. The building itself had diminutive appeal but once we passed through the narrow doorway and descended steep steps, we found ourselves in a bustling, impressive lobby. Like many city buildings in Syria, the exterior gave no hint of the scale or activity inside. The Orient House Hotel was alive with energy, as guests gathered in anticipation of a wedding the following day.

Most of the guests wore Western-style clothing, with only a few women donning elegant white silk scarfs known as hijabs. Throughout our travels in Syria, we rarely saw women in niqabs (the full-face veil covering, with only the eyes apparent). That evening, the four of us had dinner together and were again surprised by how affordable everything was – the entire meal cost just $21. As usual, we invited Taysir and Jusuf to join us but they preferred to dine separately.

Later that night, the others wandered out to explore. Denis found a barber still open at 10:30 PM, and when he asked for the price, the barber simply replied, 'Whatever you wish.' It seemed the locals were genuinely delighted to have tourists. Meanwhile, back at the hotel, a crowd had gathered in the lobby to watch El Clásico, the annual match between Barcelona and Real Madrid. By midnight, the lobby emptied as Real Madrid secured a 3-2 victory.

Denis's thoughts:

Hama

On our second evening in the country Fran and Erin joined me as I had my hair cut with great care and precision by very modern young lads who were listening to Eminem (while outside walking past were young men dressed in traditional Muslim clothing which showed Syria's diversity) and then we watched Real Madrid v Barcelona with a cheering crowd. It showed how people everywhere have so much in common. During the match two women at our table treated us to tea and chocolates.

In fact, everywhere we went in Syria people went out of their way to speak with us and offer us hospitality.

It wasn't until daylight that we truly appreciated the charm and beauty of Hama. A city of around a million people, it boasts rivers, parks and its famous ancient wooden water wheels, dating back to Roman times. On a morning walk, we became instant curiosities, warmly greeted by locals wherever we went. People thanked us for visiting their country and teenagers and families eagerly asked for selfies with us. Our little group, surrounded by enthusiastic youths, even joined in chants of 'Syria, Syria!' and football team names. Nearby, a bejewelled camel stood patiently with its keeper, ready for photo opportunities. Everyone seemed to have a cell phone, capturing the moment.

Despite advice to purchase local SIM cards before our trip, we stuck with our Vodafone cards out of convenience, and they worked surprisingly well. Over nearly a month of travelling through four different countries, the total extra cost was only about €65 each, including roaming data. Coverage was never an issue and each evening we connected to hotel Wi-Fi and stayed in touch with home via WhatsApp. Hama's charm, its welcoming people and the unexpected beauty of the city left a lasting impression.

Aleppo

The next stop on our itinerary was Syria's second-largest city – Aleppo. As we made our way north, Jusuf warned us that the highway remained a hazardous route, with sections on either side still controlled by hostile forces. For over 60 km, we sped past destroyed towns and villages – abandoned shells of concrete and steel, with no signs of life. No petrol stations, no shops, no stalls – just emptiness.

As we reached the outskirts of Aleppo, another military security cordon stopped us. Buses were emptied of passengers, and battered taxis and minibuses queued up to take travellers further into the city. Our papers were checked again before we were waved through.

Our first stop was the Aleppo Museum, a stark contrast to the devastation we had seen. The museum was open, fully intact and staffed, housing artefacts that spanned 40,000 years of history.

After a fascinating visit, our guide, Taysir, ushered us to the Aleppo Palace Hotel. Despite its name, the hotel didn't look grand from the outside but once inside, the seven-story glass building on the main square revealed its charm. We were greeted by porters in faded red blazers paired with shabby jeans and trainers, adding a quirky touch to the experience.

That night, Taysir took us to a popular falafel stand he insisted was the best in Aleppo. The long queues and buzzing atmosphere proved him right – the falafel was delicious, and the streets were lively. Families with kids, couples, groups of friends and locals on motorbikes gathered in the warm evening air. We ended the night with ice cream at a nearby shop, sitting at pavement tables, snapping selfies and recording videos to capture the joy of the moment. As the night wrapped up, we witnessed the owner collecting his takings, packing the cash into large bags – Syrian commerce in action.

The Citadel of Aleppo (Saladin's Castle)

The next morning, greeted by another sunny day, we set out to visit the Citadel of Aleppo, a towering fortress that dominates the city. Thought to be one of the oldest castles in the world, the Citadel had recently reopened after being closed for 18 months. We were only the second group to visit, walking through the gates and up the ramparts, taking in the scale of both the fortress and the war-torn city below.

From the top, the view was haunting – an endless expanse of mangled buildings, twisted steel and crumbled concrete. Homes, hotels, mosques, churches and the once-famous Souk all lay in ruins. Amid the devastation, one building stood out – a seven-story pinkish Sheraton Hotel, unscathed and still operational throughout the war. It had served as a base for journalists and TV crews, providing a stage for the war's narrative to unfold.

As we walked through the streets of what had been the Old City, the destruction felt overwhelming. Dusty rubble lined the streets, remnants of a once-thriving souk with over 1,500 shops. Taysir pointed out the ongoing reconstruction efforts, mentioning that funds were being sourced from Islamic countries to restore Aleppo's heritage.

During our exploration, a man in a red sweater approached us, inviting us to visit his shop. He shared that he hadn't seen tourists in years and, spotting us at the falafel stall, felt we were a good omen. He asked for nothing in return, simply grateful for our presence – a reminder of the past and perhaps a glimmer of hope for the future.

Restaurant in Aleppo

That afternoon, we experienced another of Taysir's favourite spots – a hidden restaurant tucked away down a side street. What looked like a garage from the outside turned out to be a simple eatery, serving freshly prepared local delicacies. It was far from glamorous but the food was delicious and the hospitality even better. Before leaving Aleppo, we passed by the historic Baron Hotel. Now boarded up and worn from war, it once hosted famous figures like Agatha Christie, who penned part of Murder on the Orient Express here, and King Faisal, who declared Syria's independence from its balcony in 1920.

Damaged Souk in Aleppo

Fran in the spotlight

Falafel cart

Traders play Backgammon

Chatting with youngsters

Erin & Fran play Backgammon

Kids in Aleppo

The famous falafel shop

Lads hanging out

Chatting with an architecture student   *Father & son in their sweet shop*

Exploring the Souks

Denis thoughts:

In Aleppo, in the shadow of the floodlit Citadel, we also went to see a wonderful band playing in a newly renovated upmarket hotel and got so swept up with it we got to our feet and danced along with the other guests (with some friendly encouragement from the manager!). I tried to dance as some of the men did – flicking my hands upwards and shaking from side to side. Some craic.

The next day we met the friendliest man you could hope to meet in the badly damaged al-Madina Souq (at 13km the largest covered historic market in the world) who treated us to tea and backgammon in a courtyard to give us rest from the midday sun. We saw the incredible treasures in the Museum of Aleppo from the Mari civilization on the Euphrates from 5,000 years ago and visited Saladin's extraordinary castle on the hill overlooking Aleppo – a perfect counterpart to the Crusader's Krak de Chevalier.

Salah ad-Din Yusuf ibn Ayyub[a] (c. 1137 – 4 March 1193), commonly known as Saladin, was the founder of the Ayyubid dynasty. Hailing from a Kurdish family, he was the first sultan of both Egypt and Syria. An important figure of the Third Crusade, he spearheaded

the Muslim military effort against the Crusader states in the Levant.
At the height of his power, the Ayyubid realm spanned Egypt, Syria,
Upper Mesopotamia, the Hejaz, Yemen, and Nubia.

Under Saladin's command, the Ayyubid army defeated the Crusaders
at the decisive Battle of Hattin in 1187, capturing Jerusalem and re-
establishing Muslim military dominance in the Levant. Although the
Crusaders' Kingdom of Jerusalem persisted until the late 13th century,
the defeat in 1187 marked a turning point in the Christian military
effort against Muslim powers in the region. Saladin died in Damascus
in 1193, having given away much of his personal wealth to his subjects;
he is buried in a mausoleum adjacent to the Umayyad Mosque.
Alongside his significance to Muslim culture, Saladin is revered
prominently in Kurdish, Turkic, and Arab culture. He has frequently
been described as the most famous Kurdish figure in history.

Morton, Nicholas (2020). The Crusader States and Their Neighbours: A Military History, 1099–1187. Oxford University Press.

It was a stark reminder of Aleppo's faded glory. Reflecting on the destruction and the city's once grand past, we couldn't help but be moved by the resilience of its people. Even amid the devastation, life continued – mosques called out for prayer and the spirit of Aleppo lives on; life, hope and the strength to rebuild.

Homs

The next morning, we checked out of our hotel and said our farewells to Aleppo. With our ever-reliable driver Jusuf at the wheel, we embarked on the 500 km journey south and back to Damascus. As we drove, we were surprised at the sparse traffic along the highway. The only notable encounter was with an International Red Cross inspection convoy. It wasn't until we neared the cities that traffic began to pick up.

Our first stop was in Homs, infamous for its role in the Syrian civil war. Once known as the birthplace of Hafez al-Assad, the father of Bashar, the city had suffered significant damage during the conflict. However, amid the devastation, the Syriac Orthodox Cathedral of the Virgin of the Belt/Girdle stood as a symbol of resilience. Although it had been damaged during the war, it has since been restored.

Praying in ancient Syriac   *Denis & Erin visiting the Mosque in Homs*

According to legend, when Saint Thomas missed Mary's assumption into Heaven, he doubted her ascension. To prove her reality, Mary gave him her leather belt (girdle) as evidence. The belt is said to have ended up in Prato Cathedral near Florence, where it is only displayed five times a year. A fragment of this sacred girdle is also believed to be housed in a special area within the cathedral in Homs.

Maaloula

Leaving Homs, we took a westward turn up the hills towards the village of Maaloula, located about 60 km from Damascus. With a population of just 7,000, Maaloula is a remote and unique place, known for being one of the last places where Aramaic is still spoken, the language used during the time of Jesus.

As we arrived, we noticed an incongruous sight: a wall poster beside the serene convent featured a fighter in army fatigues, holding an AK-47 rifle.

Denis's thoughts:

Exploring the Tranquil Beauty of Maaloula
Maaloula was one of the most serene and enchanting places I have ever visited. Nestled in a valley surrounded by hills and mountains glowing with sandy hues under the afternoon sun, the village seemed to radiate a warm, magical energy. We arrived to see a church that had been destroyed in the war but recently rebuilt.

Views of Maaloula

Our guide, a woman with limited English, welcomed us warmly and it was evident that we were the only visitors there. She led us inside the church, where we took a seat as she began to sing the Our Father in Aramaic – the very language that Jesus would have spoken. I closed my eyes, feeling connected to all those who have listened, spoken and sung these words together across the world throughout history – communities, congregations, families.

Abba,
Father,
Yəṯqadaš šəmak̲.
May thy name be holy.
Teṯe malk̲uṯak̲.
May thy kingdom come.
Tehəwe raʕuṯak̲.
May thy will be done.
Pitṯan də-ṣorak̲ hav lan yoməden.
Give us today our needed bread.
wa-Švuq lan ḥovenan.
And forgive us our debts / sins.
Hek̲ ʼənan šəvaqin lə-ḥaivenan.
As we forgive our debtors.
wə-La taʕel lan lə-nisyon.
And lead us not into temptation.
Amin.
Amen.

Translation from www.aramaicnt.org

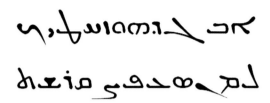

Syriac-Aramaic Alphabet (By Mathen Payyappilly Palakkappilly)

In those moments I prayed for peace: for the people of Gaza, for Palestinians everywhere, for the Israeli hostages and their families, for their leaders to find common ground, for better days to come.

Afterward, Taysir led Fran, Erin, and me on a walk through the gorge that gives Maaloula its name – meaning 'entrance.' The energy from the landscape was palpable, with its steep cliffs and a quiet, almost mystical atmosphere. A shy dog joined us, happily flopping on her side as we petted her. At one point, a teenager on a motorbike sped through the narrow passage like something out of a movie. Taysir pointed out caves in the hills, some of which had been used as dwellings and also burial sites.

Our next stop was the Convent of St. Thekla, where a small community of nuns lives. In 2013, 12 of them were kidnapped during the war but were released in a prisoner exchange two months later. The bullet holes in the religious mosaics bore silent witness to the violence that had taken place there. We climbed a series of steps winding up the rocky hillside, passing perfectly shaped pine trees along the way. The church at the top offered a breathtaking view and inside, the atmosphere was modest, yet sacred. A nun greeted us with a kind smile and handed us candles to light.

We finished our visit at the convent's gift shop, where I picked up a book on Aramaic before heading back to the van, feeling a deep sense of peace from this place.

SYRIA CRADLE OF CIVILIZATIONS

THE ANCIENT ALPHABETS

BY HANI ZA'ROURA
ARCHAEOLOGIST

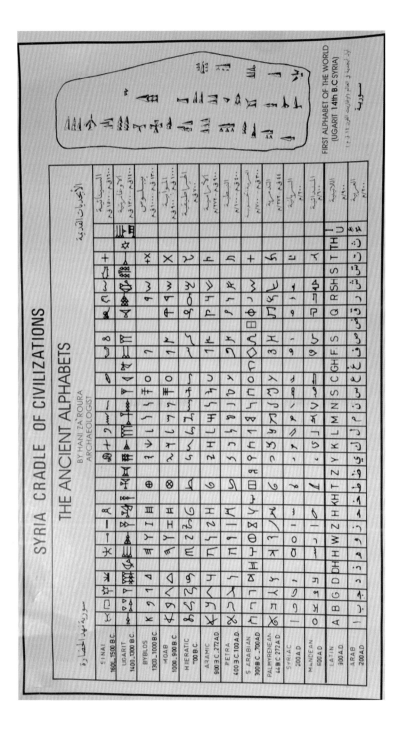

FIRST ALPHABET OF THE WORLD
(UGARIT 14th B.C SYRIA)

Damascus

The next morning, we checked out of our hotel, Aleppo Palace Hotel, and bid farewell to Aleppo, setting our sights on Damascus. With the ever-reliable Jusuf at the wheel, we set off on the nearly 400-kilometre journey south, including a stop in Homs. As before the highway was eerily quiet, with sparse traffic and only occasional signs of life. We passed an International Red Cross inspection convoy but noticed traffic only began to pick up closer to the cities.

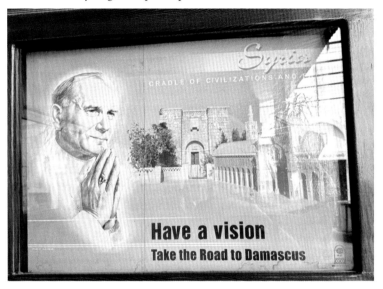

Continuing south, we arrived in Damascus. Once past the outer security cordon, the streets tightened into a maze of narrow passages where only permit-holding vehicles are allowed. The Beit Zaman was nestled in the heart of the Old City. Later that evening, we ventured out into the darkened streets, dimmed by energy rationing. We found a bustling pizza diner where the staff, all men, seemed eager to interact with us.

Denis's thoughts:

Damascus

And then there was Damascus. As we arrived at our lovely small hotel we saw hundreds and hundreds of Armenians in a parade remembering those killed in the Armenian genocide. The passionate pounding of the drums and rhythmic chanting and reverent costumes was quite unlike anything I've ever seen. A soul-shaking experience. Our tour the next day took us to the ancient Souk with spices, sweets and toys and clothes – a sensory overload. We were invited to dance with a group of men and boys dancing in a room off the Souk – so we took off our shoes and did our best. And then we went on to the famous Umayyad Mosque where Saladin's tomb is located and then to the place where St Ananias was said to have cured St Paul of his blindness after his conversion on the road to Damascus.

The narrow streets and wooden-built dwellings built over the centuries were remarkable. One of the most vibrant cities I've visited.

Remembering the victims of the Armenian genocide

Fran & Erin with Yusuf our Driver

Reflecting on a previous visit to Damascus 30 years ago. In 1994 I visited Damascus on a brief professional tourism scoping assignment arising from the Middle East Peace process at that time. I was keen to revisit the landmarks that had stayed with me: the 2,000-year-old Souk, the street called Straight, and the Citadel. Unfortunately, I learned that the Citadel had been closed to the public for decades, restricted only to military access – a stark reminder of its continued strategic importance despite modern advancements.

The Souk of Damascus

Dancing in Damascus

The Damascus Souk remains a vibrant hub, with its 700 stalls offering everything from traditional shops to makeshift stands. The market, an enduring symbol of commerce and life, has been a vital part of the city for millennia.

Just around the corner stood the Umayyad Mosque, the fourth holiest site in Islam. Inside, we removed our shoes and donned appropriate attire. The mosque's Mausoleum, which houses the graves of Saladin and his brother, was an evocative site. Recently, Saladin's tomb had been joined by Imam Saeed Ramadan Al Bouti, a Sunni scholar of world renown whose violent death, inside the mosque during the civil war, made him a martyr. Differing accounts have him dying in a suicide bomb blast or being shot dead immediately after the explosion.) The Umayyad Mosque's architectural splendour was awe-inspiring. The main hall, filled with Persian rugs, can accommodate up to 20,000 worshippers. Men prayed silently in the centre while women and children were sectioned off. Shrines within the mosque marked the burial place of John the Baptist's head and Muhammad's martyred grandson.

In the afternoon, Denis and I indulged in a traditional Hammam experience at Hamman Albakri, a men-only Turkish bath integral to Islamic culture. The process included various steam rooms, massages, and a thorough cleansing. Despite the physical intensity, we emerged feeling revitalised. That evening, we discovered a rooftop restaurant adjacent to our hotel. The retro-faded style of the place did not reflect its value for money; our dinner bill for four, including drinks, totalled just $48. The experience was both charming and economical.

Denis's thoughts:

The hammam experience with Dad was fantastic, very different from an Irish spa treatment! The care the masseurs gave to each of us was much needed as they were laid face down on the wet tiled floor with men chattering everywhere pouring cold water on themselves, and steam billowing all around us. Everyone was interested in saying hi and greeting us with a smile and a welcome. It was cool to see how Syrian men chilled out and then sat around chatting and drinking tea.

At dinner that night we had a hard time trying to count out the blocks of cash we needed to pay and then all collapsed into giggles as we spilled the money on the floor and had to start counting again. We had yet to develop the slick counting skills that we saw the locals use. Erin, Fran and I went for a drink that night and saw many chic and trendy young people out to socialise and met a DJ who was about to play a gig at a restaurant beautifully bathed in lights strung around trees. He told me we were the first tourists he had met in over 12 years. He said things were very tough for him and his friends (and for Christians in general), and he hoped to leave if they could.

Shop front in Damascus

Light & shade in Damascus

A tea-seller in traditional costume

Fruits for sale

Three generations

Ladies smoking shisha

Lady in charge of the WC

Erin makes new friends

A nice break for refreshments

A coffin maker in Damascus

Erin & Fran meeting students in Damascus

A young couple stop to chat with us

Narrow streets with overhanging buildings

A candle-maker at work

The only 5-star hotel in Damascus

On our final morning, Denis and I took a quiet walk around the city, noting the serenity of a Saturday. Near the Iranian Embassy, we saw the remnants of an annex recently destroyed by an Israeli bombing – a reminder of the precise nature of modern conflict. As we returned to our hotel, we met an Irish man working with the UN in Damascus. His presence would have been a valuable resource earlier in our journey.

Reflecting on our conversations with Taysir and Jusuf, I inquired about their lives and careers in the aftermath of the war. Taysir shared with a trembling voice, 'Before the war, I was a millionaire. Now, with rampant inflation and the loss of all our savings, we manage as best we can with retirement funds and support from friends and family.' Despite the hardship, his pride and resilience were evident.

Chatting with passers-by

Delicious Pistachio ice-cream

Taysir & Dermod chat together

The Syrian people

Our visit to Syria left a profound impact on all of us. From the moment we arrived, we were embraced with warmth and hospitality everywhere we went. There was no probing curiosity – just genuine gratitude that we, as outsiders, took the time to explore their country. Everywhere, from the bustling streets to the quiet villages, we were met with humour and friendliness. The Syrians we encountered, whether in the north, south, east or west, were cheerful and welcoming in ways we hadn't anticipated. It wasn't just a show for a few foreign visitors; it was simply their way of being.

Despite the horrors and challenges they have faced – war, genocide, poverty and the recent projection by PBS that over 16 million Syrians will need humanitarian assistance, the highest number since 2011 – the people we met were remarkably resilient. They maintain a sense of pride, optimism and generosity that is both extraordinary and inspiring.

As our time in Syria drew to a close, we boarded the fancy van that had brought us here and prepared for the journey back to Beirut. Our first stop was to exchange any remaining Syrian currency for dollars – a small amount, just $3, in my case.

Sadly, we had to say goodbye to our wonderful fellow travellers, Erin and Francesca. Erin was off to catch a flight, and Francesca would depart the following day. We had shared many memorable moments and as we parted, we set up a WhatsApp group and a shared photo Dropbox, promising to stay in touch and plan future adventures together. Erin has since published a travel article about our trip.

Syria, though largely forgotten and isolated on the global stage, is a country that still holds immense significance. While many have moved on, the tragedy of Syria's situation remains, and the country is often overlooked due to its limited strategic or resource importance. We felt privileged to experience Syria in its current, lived reality. We were not bloggers or vloggers tasked with promoting the country; we were simply visitors from Ireland who saw its unique beauty and spirit firsthand.

The Syrian People truly deserve a brighter future.

Erin's account of Syria:

'Travelling to Syria was a surreal and unforgettable experience. History has always fascinated me; I have heard many wonderful things about the culture. So, when I could travel to Syria, I immediately signed up.

I sometimes travel to destinations deemed 'unsafe' and 'scary' by Western media because it's a chance to show others that these places aren't so scary. It is also a way to highlight the culture, the places, and the people. After all, we are all human.

I knew going on this trip was risky because of turmoil in nearby countries, but I trusted our tour company, which said our safety was paramount. So, if the tour was still happening, I was still going.

So many things stand out, making this such an incredible trip. I would say first, the group that I was with. There were four of us, and we immediately clicked. We learned that a few more were supposed to join us but they cancelled. So, we bonded because we all had similar reasons for wanting to visit, especially since Syria had been closed off to tourists for years.

A group can make or break a trip and our group of being up for an adventure was always game for anything. There was also never a shortage of laughter.

We visited incredible sites, so it's hard to say a favourite because they were all unique in their own way. Krak de Chevaliers was spectacular and grand. The outside doesn't look like a castle, but upon entering, there are so many rooms and corners to look at that it's easy to get lost inside. The views of the farms from the top made one feel like you're in Southeast Asia.

While driving to Palmyra, it was hard not to see the destruction from the war. The rubble on the ground from the remains of homes was something else. We learned that about 10,000 are still here but once 60,000 people lived here.

Upon arriving at the ancient city, our guide, Taysir, showed us postcards of Palmyra's appearance before the war. Seeing how grand this city was and seeing lots of rubble on the ground was sad. But, while it was tragic, it was still amazing to see the remains of Roman-style columns and walk around what would have been one of the biggest temples in the Orient.

Another thing that stood out was talking with locals. Some told us that they hadn't seen tourists in over seven years. Others thanked us for visiting. We also had a lot of selfies, which was great.

Tasir told us to encourage others to come here and let everyone know the country is safe. I would have to agree with him. For those wanting to get out of their comfort zones and witness incredible history, Syria is a place to visit.'

Erin has since published a travel article on our trip: Travel to Syria with Untamed Borders

confettitravelcafe.com/travel-to-syria-with-untamed-borders

Our favourite billboard ad in Syria

Francesca's account of Syria:

'The highlight of my trip to Syria – by far – were the people. Both the people I travelled to Syria with but also the people I met in Syria. The kindness that was radiated to us by the people I met still sticks with me to this day. It's the one thing I always go on about when people ask me 'How was Syria?' Everyone was so curious about why we were there, why we chose Syria out of all places in the world to travel to. Everyone we met kindly gave us tea or treats from their shop and invited us into their shops and homes to have a conversation. It's what I'll remember most of my trip.

The most memorable parts of Syria were the everyday 'normal' moments. I remember singing along to Eminem songs with local boys in a barber shop as Denis was getting his hair trimmed. I remember being on the edge of my seat at the hotel we were staying at, watching the Madrid vs Barcelona game play out with all of the other guests (mostly Syrian, I assume). Madrid won and the entire room jumped to their feet and roared with glee. I remember a girl waving to me at an ice cream shop to catch my attention and then making a heart with her hands. We had never met before. She had never seen me before but she immediately radiated warmth and love. I'm lucky I got to catch that moment on camera so I can look back at it for years to come. It's the little moments I remember most about Syria.

The entire city of Damascus was the most interesting part of the trip for me. I learned before the trip that Damascus is one of the oldest continually inhabited capitals of the world and being able to walk through over 8,000 years of history was unlike anything I've ever experienced. From the Umayyad Mosque, to the palaces and to the old souks, the city was dripping in history and it requires an entire trip all on its own to truly take it all in

I choose to travel to places that are off the beaten track because there's often so little information on these countries and I feel I owe it to these countries to explore all of what they have to offer. It's also a thrill for me to see places so few people get the privilege to travel to, through my own eyes. I then get to share my experience with friends, family members and anyone that follows me on social media as I share my travel stories.

Travelling to Syria has made me question what I see in the news more. I purposely decided to travel to Syria to see what the country was like for myself. I already didn't believe the news' narrative on Syria simply being a 'war torn country' and I was proven right. It's so much more than that. If you travel to Syria, you'll see how the people have rebuilt their cities and their country. They are resilient. They are hopeful. They are kind and welcoming. This is the side of Syria that the news doesn't show. The human side. Travelling to Syria makes me want to travel to other lesser travelled to, and often misunderstood, places so that I can form my own opinions and not simply believe what the media is feeding me.

So, when people ask me, "How was Syria?" It is not as simple to answer, as "it was amazing!"

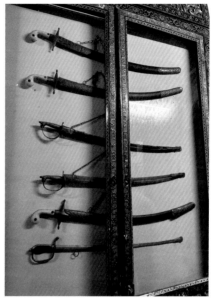

Chatting with a German tourist   *Swords made with Damascus steel*

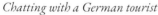

Denis's thoughts on Syria:

Taysir was the most extraordinary guide – his love for his country radiated through him and energised anyone in his company. He also told me one of the most profound things I've ever heard when he asked us – when is a human being at their happiest? The answer was – the moments they are relieving themselves after urgently needing the toilet. As a man who inherited his father's bladder and experiences such urgent moments frequently, this certainly rang true for me and I remember his words regularly! Yusuf the Driver had a very friendly demeanour and communicated with smiles and handshakes. And playing Umm Kulthum (the Voice of Egypt) songs for us as we drove! Syrians are amongst the friendliest and most welcoming people I have ever met anywhere. They showed no bitterness or resentment despite the utter devastation they have suffered. The level of destruction is indescribable, caused largely by indiscriminate bombings of huge swathes of the country by Russian planes. The Bashar Al Assad regime had shown promise in its early years, but when faced with mass protests calling for reforms in 2011, he responded savagely against his own people with Russian assistance. Over 600,000 people have been killed and many millions have fled.

But it is not the destruction that stayed with me most after our visit – rather the wonders of the ancient land – both natural wonders and those created by many marvellous civilisations over thousands of years. We also had so much fun. Erin and Fran were perfect travel companions, and we had a great laugh along the way. I could understand why Dad had been so taken with the country on his visit there in the 90s, and it was nice that he wanted to share it with me.

I loved our visit to Syria. Although the country had suffered unimaginable tragedy in recent times, the spirit and resilience of the people and the opportunities for tourism and trade gave me hope that they may have a brighter future. The Syrian people's attitude and love of life is humbling and inspiring. However, rights for women are still far behind those in Ireland. For example, Erin and Fran could not dance with us when we danced as it would not be seen as appropriate. As men we were not supposed to shake hands with women. Certain professions are thought to be only appropriate for men. The country still has a long way to go, but Ireland was a very different place just 50 years ago, so perhaps there is hope that Syria can progress quickly also in terms of gender equality. And Syria is a place where many different religions and places of worship coexist peacefully side-by-side. It is not to say there is no friction at times (and we only saw a small slice), but from what we could see and hear it was encouraging to see a high degree of tolerance between faiths in the country (The main faith groups in Syria are Sunni 74%, Alawi Shia Muslim 11.5%, Christian 8.9%, Druze 3%, Ismaili Shia Muslim 1%).

A busker injured in the war

Saying goodbye to our group

Taysir Our Syrian Guide:

My name is Taysir, I was born in Damascus and am a Palestinian Syrian citizen – my family emigrated from Palestine to Syria in 1948. After school I studied in Hotel & Tourism Training Centre Institute and graduated in 1984. I have worked as a guide ever since then.

When people ask me why I became a guide, it makes me remember. Firstly, I love speaking with people in different languages and I studied French, German, Italian, Japanese, Arabic, English. I love languages and people.

I also love tourism and showing people the natural landscapes of Syria – like desert, mountains, valleys, rivers and the ruins of marvelous civilisations that came before us. We have about 10,000 archaeological sites in Syria. The highlights are about 100, and the most important are about 30 -35 sites. These are the things that helped me to choose this job and to deal with people and offer them an amazing experience in Syria. It is fascinating for me to understand their mentalities and their cultures and every tour is a completely new experience for me as I see my country all over again in different ways through their eyes and their minds. And also to learn about their lives in other parts of the world.

I enjoy everything about being a guide. Damascus – the ancient city – is like an open-air active museum. And the genuine nature of the Syrian people – we are a very emotional people, and also cooperative at the same time.

In terms of the sites I most enjoy, I would say nature mixed with ruins. Many of our most interesting sites are situated in a special area – like Palmyra in the beautiful desert on the Silk Road built by the Palmyran civilisation, or Krak de Chevaliers (the most well preserved Crusader castle in the world) which is situated in a green area with rivers and valleys. Or Saladin's castle in a strategic area on a mountainous ridge between two deep ravines and surrounded by a forest, or the busy souk of Aleppo which are 12km long and date from 12th century and the city itself which is one of the oldest continuously occupied cities in the world. Or Ugarit, the site of the first alphabet in the world from 1400BC. And Maloula in the sandy rocky hills where people are still speaking the Aramaic language spoken by Jesus – one of the last places in the world you can hear it.

We have so many places I love! It is difficult to choose a favourite! One of the most important is the amphitheatre at Busra which is considered one of the most important in the world. In Damascus there is the monastery / convent dedicated to Virgin Mary with an icon believed to be painted by St. Luke! One of the oldest churches in the world which was used underground in a cave from 59AD. The dead cities with 1,200 churches from 2-6 century. The Euphrates area with the famous site of Mari dating back to 3,000BC and one of the most important archaeological sites in the world. And then there is the Euphrates River itself where so many of the earliest villages on Earth were established around 7000BC – the Cradle of Civilisation. And more and more and more, so many! Too many to write all now!

Anyway, thanks to God I have the opportunity to do this job for so many years and with luck to keep doing it for a long time to come! As you can see, I am very proud of my country! And finally, wiishing blessings to you and your father from all my heart.

Back to Beirut Airport

The taxi ride back to the airport in the morning was just $20. Once we arrived, we were met with layer upon layer of security checks and baggage screenings. After clearing passport control, I faced yet another inspection of my backpack by the military.

It was my metal, expandable walking pole that caught their attention. The pole, which had been essential throughout the trip – helping me navigate broken sidewalks, climb ancient ruins and acting as a virtual third hand – was flagged. They put it through the scanner twice and soon an officer with gold and silver decorations arrived, eyeing it with suspicion. He twirled the pole in his hand, the sharp tip on full display and said firmly, 'No sir, you cannot take this with you.'

I wasn't ready to give up so easily. That stick had been my steady balance companion, and I wasn't about to let it be confiscated at the final leg of the Lebanon journey. I protested, pleading my case, even shamelessly playing the *age* card. After a moment of consideration, the officer relented and handed it back with a smile. With my trusty pole in hand, we boarded the flight home, feeling triumphant.

JORDAN

Jordan (/ˈdʒɔrdən/;
Arabic:الأردن al-Urdun),
officially the Hashemite
Kingdom of Jordan

Arriving in Amman: The Gateway to Jordan

We touched down at Queen Alia International Airport in Amman, Jordan, where the usual arrival process went smoothly. As soon as we cleared customs, we were greeted by a representative from Atlas Travel – a company we had only secured a guide from the night before, given the uncertainty of our plans. He swiftly handled the arrival tax for $60, helped with our luggage and suggested we exchange some currency before leading us outside to meet our driver.

Our destination was Jerash, where we would link up with our new guide. As we skirted the edges of Amman, I was taken aback by something unexpected: rows and rows of roadside garden centres. In a land more famous for its deserts, the abundance of greenery felt counterintuitive. But Jordan, as I was quickly reminded, is a land of surprises – and still surprisingly fertile.

The ancient thoroughfare in Jerash

Jerash

After locking in our dates for Jordan, a friend suggested we reach out to Ireland's embassy in Amman for advice. When we did, a senior official strongly encouraged us to visit the ancient city of Jerash. Little did we know, Jerash was already the first stop on our itinerary. Our driver dropped us off in a car park, where we were introduced to our guide, Amer Nizami Bani Mustafa – the ninth generation of his family to live in Jerash.

With his quirky hat, stylish sunglasses and fashionable khaki outfit, Amer exuded confidence and professionalism from the start. Born and raised in Jerash, his family's roots in the city span nine generations. As soon as we met him, he took command of the tour and every day under his guidance, we learned more than we could have ever expected about this remarkable place.

Denis's thoughts:

We were met by our driver Abdelsalem who took us to Jerash to meet our guide Amer. Amer was as engaging a guide as you could hope to meet. He had studied religious texts in Islam, Christianity and Judaism. He was funny, irreverent, knowledgeable and warm – simultaneously. He brought history to life with his stories. Sometimes simplified but always with a view to helping his listeners to understand the various threads and strands that woven together made the patchwork quilt of histories and cultures in these lands. He made us aware of the profound nature of the events that took place in the land of Jordan but demystified it all by providing analogies we could digest. And he had some great one-liners – for example when speaking of the foolishness of suicide bombers seeking rewards in Heaven, he said – 'I don't want 72 virgins, give me one expert any day.'

A mer explained that the reason Arab homes are often so large is because multiple generations live together under one roof. When a man marries, his new wife traditionally moves into the family home – a reflection of deep-rooted tribal customs and the importance of maintaining the bloodline. Our next five days with Amer felt like being part of an engaging one-man play. Attentive, serious, witty and irreverent, he was full of energy. Though he smoked, it was nowhere near the chain-smoking levels of our previous guides, Taysir and Jusuf.

Amer had never been to Syria, deeming it currently unsafe, but he didn't rule out a future visit. As for Israel, he had never been and didn't plan to go, citing historical reasons. He explained that, traditionally, Arabs didn't recognise borders. Nomadic tribes roamed freely across an amorphous region known as the Sham, the 7th century caliphate, or religious/military region spanning parts of modern-day Egypt, Palestine, Jordan, Syria, and Iraq. This area was once common land for tribes to follow their flocks, with borders becoming relevant only after modern states were established. Cities like Jerash, Amer told us, had been ruled by various powers – Egyptian, Greek, Roman – each adapting the architecture and culture to their own needs.

The ancient ruins of Jerash are remarkably well-preserved, enclosed within the once-imposing protective walls of the modern city that bears its name. We began our tour at the grand Hadrian Gate, starting a two-hour walk through what was once a thriving Roman metropolis. Jerash is considered one of the best-preserved Roman cities in the world, showcasing the innovations of the empire: wide streets, theatres, colonnades, public baths, forums and sophisticated water and waste systems.

Amer added that the people who lived here were of the Semitic Arabic race – a race, not a religion. 'We are the brownies of the Middle East,' he joked, explaining that tribe lineage is traced through the maternal line. In line with this tradition, women keep their family names after marriage rather than adopting their husband's name. As we wrapped up our memorable visit to Jerash, Amer proudly shared that he had personally guided the then Prince Charles and Duchess Camilla, and now King Charles and Queen Camilla when they visited the city in November 2021.

During our long drive, we asked Amer about the recent tit-for-tat airstrikes between Iran and Israel. On April 13, 2023, Iran launched (slow) drones, cruise and ballistic missiles toward Israel and the Israeli-occupied Golan Heights. Israel retaliated six days later, on April 19, with airstrikes targeting an air defence facility near Isfahan in central Iran.

We had heard rumours that the Jordanian air force had intercepted and shot down several Iranian drones as they crossed into Jordanian airspace. Amer mentioned that a cousin of his, who works with civil defence in a small Jordanian village, had witnessed several downed missiles crashing nearby. Strangely, when they were examined, none carried bombs or warheads. If true, it seemed like a bizarre *mock pillow fight* between two nations – a symbolic warning without real intent to cause damage.

Arriving in Petra

Keeping up with the Joneses   *Dermod & friends*

Petra and Little Petra

Back in the car, we set off on a long journey to our next UNESCO world heritage site: the legendary Petra, dating back to the first century AD. It is located roughly halfway between Amman and Aqaba and is one of Jordan's most renowned landmarks. We drove south along the Aqaba motorway, with the sun setting to the west, casting a warm glow over the stark, lunar-like landscape. We made a quick stop at a food complex along the motorway. It was just Denis and me now, and we already missed our companions, Erin and Francesca. Like in Lebanon and Syria, our guide and driver preferred to eat separately, leaving us as the only diners in a massive complex that could easily accommodate hundreds. The manager explained that they had barely seen any tourists since October 2023. Tourism is a significant industry in Jordan, especially in its upscale market, so the impact of this drop in visitors must have been immense. Prices in Jordan also reflected its position as a higher-end destination – at our Dead Sea hotel, for example, two small beers and sandwiches set us back $76, before the tip.

As night fell, we left the highway and navigated smaller, poorly lit roads that wound through a few hilly villages. Eventually, we reached the town of Wadi Musa, the gateway to Petra, where Eastern traditions meet Hellenistic architecture. We were staying overnight at the Movenpick Resort Petra, a five-star hotel conveniently located across from the newly constructed Petra Museum. The hotel's entrance and car park were well-guarded, with metal ramps, barriers and security personnel. Our bags were screened twice at check-in, a reminder of the high security measures in place.

The next morning, breakfast proved that five-star status wasn't just for show. The buffet was an impressive spread of fresh fruits of every sort, shape, size and colour, every imaginable combination of nuts, cereals, breads, cold meats, salads, cheeses, freshly prepared omelettes and much more options and the attentive, polite staff made sure we had everything we needed. With only about twenty guests in the hotel – mainly Belgians, Germans and a couple of Americans – there seemed to be more staff than visitors. The dining room overlooked a serene pool, a welcome respite after a long day of travel or sightseeing.

At 9:30 a.m., Amer arrived to take us across to the Petra Visitor Centre. The morning was already bright and hot as we walked up the hill to the right, passing rows of spotless yellow taxis neatly parked, with drivers standing by. No business and little hope for any. It seemed the high level of compliance and availability required for taxi licences in Petra kept the drivers diligently at their posts, even in the absence of tourists.

Entering Petra through a 1.2km gorge   *In front of The Treasury*

There are three ways to travel the three kilometres into the UNESCO protected Petra – walk, ride a horse for just one kilometre like Indiana Jones or travel in a nice, covered golf cart. We paid the round ticket fare for the cart. I never used the return fare – I walked back. It was remarkable that so few people were around. Entrance to the ancient site is through the Al Siq Canyon which is 1.2km in length. Emerging from the relatively dark, shaded canyon into the bright sunlight with Petra's Treasury Building revealed in front of you, cannot be described as anything less than breath-taking. It was the Nabataean Arabs who carved this wondrous place out of rock. The entire complex is hidden away. Petra indeed merits its nomination as one of the Seven Wonders of the World.

Amer in full flow

Rock formations in Petra

We had coffee inside and Amer gave an exceptional solo performance (which I recorded) describing the myth, the mystery and historical accuracy of the ancient Nabatean Empire. The story of Salome was acted and told by Amer with the backdrop of Petra. An outstanding performance. We took photos, far and wide. Denis petted wild cats, dogs and two dressed up, selfie-ready camels. We walked, we climbed, we stopped into caves, and discovered water caverns. It went on and on. It was past midday; I was getting tired.

I retreated slowly through the welcome shade of the canyon. Amer and Denis went on for hours. Denis climbed the 850 steps to the Monastery al-Deir. 'Hard going even for the fit,' said the guidebooks. He bought a keyring from a vendor, with a soft camel attached at the top. It hangs now in our kitchen.

The only fate of our entire adventure happened that evening when I banged my knee against the side of the bath. At the time it didn't feel too bad. By dinnertime, in the hotel's fancy rooftop restaurant overlooking Petra, I was in pain. My knee had swelled to the size of an orange. I asked the waiter for a bag of ice, I then rolled up my trousers and held the ice pack unsophisticated in place for the duration of the meal. Meanwhile a musician playing a guitar, crooned country and western songs.

In the morning Denis and I visited the stunning new museum. The building is a low-lying, sleek, minimalist floating design of 2,300sm by the Japanese architectural office of Yamashita Sekkei Inc. and paid for with $7 Million USD by the Japanese Government. It was only officially opened in 2021. It contains models, diagrams, audio-visual and multi-modal interpretations. It is a wonderful presentation and interpretation – professional and restrained. Outside the clean lines of the structure floated on a surrounding moat.

Afterwards, Amer called us – time to leave.

Petra to the Dead Sea

'We are now heading north,' Amer told us. 'We are not going near the highway – we are taking the Wadi Arabia scenic route up into the mountains and then down to the Dead Sea.'

Our first stop, about 20 km north, was the site of Little Petra. Like Petra – another city carved into the mountains. It acted as the inland holding port for the caravans with all their goods traversing the Silk Road. The officials from main Petra wouldn't let unchecked merchants into the city. They were examined here first in Little Petra. Animals were rested, fed and watered. Goods itemised and taxes levied. The merchants then invited back to Petra, paid their dues at the Treasury. Petra offered protection, sustenance, rest and relaxation before the caravans moved on. We had a Turkish coffee which is certainly an acquired taste.

Puppies at Little Petra

Back in the car, we headed up into the mountains. The road twisted and turned higher and higher, with no other traffic. After about an hour we stopped at a wayside shop perched at the top. We needed to use the facilities – the squat variety. In the large shop, we spoke to the owner who told us a family of 19 was dependent on the business. Once again, we were the only customers. We sat having a coffee by the open window looking at the magnificent valley spread out for hundreds of kilometres below us.

Jordanian desertscapes

Pointing out a desert region below, Amer explained that this was the route that Moses took to lead the tribes of Israel out of Egypt and into the Promised Land. The desert below, according to Amer, was where they wandered for forty years! Justly, as we descended and drove through the scrubland and emerged near the Dead Sea, we agreed that it wasn't that vast. Clearly, Moses and his pals had a poor sense of direction.

As we descended from the mountains toward the Dead Sea, we passed by towering mounds of gleaming white stone. These were part of an active open-cast potash mine, a fascinating contrast to the barren landscape. Potash, a key component of fertilisers, is rich in potassium salts that are soluble in water. The most common form, potassium chloride, is not only used to boost soil fertility but also has a range of applications in medicine, chemical manufacturing and even as a salt substitute in food. The Arab Potash Company (APC), which operates here, is the sole producer of potash in the Arab world.

Maybe that's what Moses discovered.

Denis's thoughts on Petra:

Petra actually exceeded my expectations. It was a place I had hoped to visit since I was a boy watching Indiana Jones. Entering the site through a 1.2km gorge with Dad and Amer was a breathtaking experience. There were very few tourists compared to normal times which made things less stressful (but also left me with a tinge of sadness for the reason it was so quiet and guilt that we were there at all). The city was built over 2,000 years ago by the Nabataean people who were an Arabic nomad tribe who had become amazing traders and business people buying and selling goods at the intersection between the Silk Road, the Levant, Europe and Africa. They chose to build their main city at Petra because it was completely defendable.

Stop Wars

River of light   *Tourists make the heart sign*

The building everyone recognises is called the Treasury – it is the first thing you see when you come through the gorge. It was decorated with statues of Gods from many different faiths and civilisations – a way of telling visiting traders that everyone is welcome here. There were camels and dogs and cats which all added to the experience – surreal and normal at the same time. It was very special to be there with Dad. When you venture beyond the Treasury, there are dozens and dozens of buildings of different sizes, as well as hundreds of caves – some natural and some man made. The colour of the rock in the caves was magical – swirls and splotches of nature's designs in red, and crimson and orange and beige and all sorts of indescribable shades and tones. After Dad decided to sensibly go back to the hotel and out of the midday sun, I went wandering up a long climb to 'the Monastery'. The views were spectacular. I chatted with a variety of traders and tourists and had little encounters with many dogs and cats and donkeys.

When I arrived back at the hotel later that afternoon, it had been a long day. I met a group of Korean tourists who asked me to take their picture as they made the heart sign with their fingers. I went to see the museum that afternoon and again the next morning with Dad. The building was a stunning design, and we marvelled at the achievements of the Nabataeans and other civilisations of that time in helping spread trade and culture and skills – which helped create the world we know today.

The next morning we set off from Petra towards the Dead Sea, stopping off first at little Petra – a place where the Nabataeans welcomed trade delegations and conducted customs checks. The manmade and natural caves were more cream-coloured than those in Petra itself, and the effect of the gorge and rock faces was very calming.

Then we drove along a road cutting through stunning rock formations. Amer told us that this was the road that Moses and the Israelites took on their way from Egypt. It was more lush with vegetation than I might have imagined. Then we arrived at the desert where they were lost for 40 years – but not literally he told us. They were spiritually lost, not yet ready to earn their promised land.

He proceeded then to tell us about the tale at the centre of all three faiths – from Abraham to Jacob and the 12 sons to Joseph escaping to Egypt and becoming rich and successful and his brothers joining him there. Until they were resented and taken into captivity and slavery.

He told us about the modern-day schism between the King of Jordan and his brother who he had put under house arrest. Stories about the Quraysh tribe into which Muhammad was born and the Hashemite tribe from whence the modern rulers of Jordan emerged, were intriguing. Both tribes had been part of the movement that came together to fight under Prince Faisal against the Turks in the First World War. *(A somewhat inaccurate version of which was told in the famous film Lawrence of Arabia which tells one perspective of the story of T.E. Lawrence's efforts to unite and fight with the Arab tribes to defeat the Turks. Proving the William Faulkner quote that 'the past is never dead, it's not even past' to be true, since the fall of the Assad regime, the Sykes-Picot Agreement of 1916 has been in the news again. This treaty – which betrayed the Arabs and left Lawrence disillusioned and depressed – divided what is now Syria between the French and British and stymied nascent efforts by the Arabs to build a fledgling democratic state of their own. The ramifications of this agreement are being felt to this day.)*

Prince Faisal in the front, with T.E. Lawrence (of Arabia) behind his left shoulder, at the Paris Peace Conference in 1919 (photographer unknown)

Dad and I were both fascinated with these stories told so well – in the places where they had happened. One of the most interesting journeys I've ever taken.

The Easter Bunny at the Kempinski Hotel

Dead Sea

We finally arrived at our next hotel, the Kempinski Hotel Ishtar Dead Sea. Similar to our previous destination in Jordan, we arrived through manned security gates and our bags were screened and searched. A sign at the entrance door said: OUTSIDE FOOD, BEVERAGES, HUBBLY BUBBLY ARE NOT PERMITTED INSIDE THE HOTEL.

The hotel complex is fabulous. Large bedrooms with private covered terraces, private beach cottages, several restaurants, enormous pillar-less 30-metre-high glass walls looking out over the Dead Sea. Amenities, gyms, pools and a team of hundreds of well-trained courteous staff. In the distance is Israel and in between the still waters of The Dead Sea.

Denis's thoughts:

I asked Amer if there were any plants or fish in the Dead Sea. 'No,' he replied, 'that's why it's called the Dead Sea.' Not the brightest question I have ever asked!

After checking in, I made my way straight to the sea. I had missed my daily swim since leaving Wicklow and I eagerly stripped off down to my togs and my spirits soared as I plunged face first into the sea relishing my first dip for over ten days... OWWW... NOO... My eyes stung like they'd been pepper sprayed! I tried to wipe them with my wet salty hands which only made them worse. How could I have been such a fool to have forgotten that the Dead Sea is eight times saltier than a normal sea!!!!! The pain lasted about four minutes as I lay floating on the sea not wanting anyone to see what an eejit I was before I could open them again and make my way towards the shower to wash them with clean water. I then had my body massaged from head to toe with Dead Sea mud full of minerals by a very friendly

Palestinian man who was working there. I had to then stand for ten minutes caked in mud as it worked its magic before showering off and then getting back in the sea to enjoy a good float – this time eyes looking upwards! It's such a surreal experience. I felt like a new man afterwards. The days of travel and staying in different beds most nights had left us both tired and it was great to be pampered and switch off for a little while.

No sooner had we settled into our rooms when I received a message from our previous hotel informing me that I had left my passport and cash in the room safe. After a quick arrangement to cover courier costs, the items were personally returned to me the very next day – a level of service that truly impressed me.

The next morning, we were greeted by yet another stunning breakfast buffet. One section featured an array of about 20 different types of donuts in every colour of the rainbow – red, pink, blue, yellow – each in varying shapes and sizes. Despite the hotel having over 200 rooms, plus villas and beach cottages, it seemed there were no more than 40 guests staying, all served by a dedicated staff of at least 300.

We had dinner and decided to order the Chef's special. After a 40-minute wait (and I admit, I was quite hungry by then), I casually mentioned the delay. This triggered a flurry of activity. Soon, three gentlemen arrived at our table – Chef Bakeet, Maitre'd Mr. Momen, and head waiter Moha Qtaishat – armed with a card signed by all of them. They were deeply apologetic, explaining they were facing technical issues in the kitchen and had just launched a new menu. Their sincerity was evident and after wishing them well with the new menu, the atmosphere was quickly restored to harmony.

The next morning, I opted out of another tour. While Amer, the driver, and Denis went off to explore ancient ruins and visit the site of Jesus' baptism in the Jordan River, I decided to head for the beach. Well, a very different kind of beach – the Dead Sea.

My visit to the Dead Sea was quite the experience. The hotel had its own private section, marked by parasols, deck chairs, showers and attendants. I was advised to start with a 15-minute soak in the water. Cautiously, I waded in, joining four other guests already floating. Within moments, I made the novice mistake of rubbing my eyes with a wet hand – instantly, my eyes stung like fire. Clambering out, I rushed up the path, trying to clear my vision.

An attendant appeared with a large bucket of black mud and before I knew it, I was covered from head to toe. My back, front, head, arms and feet were all slathered in thick, gooey mud. It felt strange but oddly therapeutic. He instructed me to go back into the water and let the mud work its magic for 25 minutes. I complied, sinking into the salty waters once more.

A Belgian couple, also coated in black mud, sat down beside me. It was their first time in Jordan, likely recent retirees, and we chatted about our experiences, remarking on the strange sensation of being among the few tourists in the country.

After letting the mud do its thing, I floated effortlessly in the Dead Sea, allowing the minerals to work their wonders. When it was time to rinse off, it took a long, thorough scrub to wash most of it away. An attendant then hosed off the stubborn bits and gave me a standing salt massage, followed by more rinsing.

By the time I changed and returned to the main building, I felt completely relaxed, cleansed, and rejuvenated. A dip in the Dead Sea is an unforgettable experience and at that precise moment, life felt good.

Dad does his stretches

That evening, Denis and I headed to the lower bar area to enjoy a sundowner. As we raised our glasses to toast the sunset over the Dead Sea, it felt magical – the sky painted in hues of orange and pink as the sun dipped below the horizon.

Later that night, we were treated to live entertainment on the open-air terrace, featuring a captivating performance by a renowned belly dancer accompanied by a pianist. The performance was truly special and brought back memories of a few days before my trip when my wife and I visited a local Lebanese restaurant in Greystones where we live. That night, we had stumbled upon their weekly belly dancing evening, complete with local dancers and lively music.

Denis's account of his tour – Day Trip in the footsteps of the Prophets

I went with Amber and Abdelsalem on a tour to the place where John the Baptist baptised Jesus in the River Jordan and then to Mt. Nebo, where Moses first saw the Promised Land before he died. I was fascinated by the opportunity to visit such sites of historical, Christian, spiritual and cosmic significance.

Mosaic of the baptism of Jesus *The baptismal site of Jesus*

The River Jordan separating Israel & Jordan

Baptism Site of Jesus Christ – 'Bethany Beyond the Jordan' – Al-Maghtas

Al-Maghtas is the Arabic word for a site of immersion and implicitly of baptism. Immersion tends to mean something very different to Irish people!

We arrived at the visitor centre where there was one tour bus with a group from Italy. On the walls were photos of many world leaders who had visited the site, including Ireland's former President Mary McAleese. We walked side by side down the beautifully laid path through the small forest. Amer pointed out a small waterflow said to be where John the Baptist washed when he lived in the wilderness – I knelt down and washed my face clean. John had lived in the wild, bearded and eating honey, wearing animal clothes and sleeping in a cave – making enemies of the powerful as he spoke of a Kingdom of the spirit far greater than theirs.

The fourth gospel (The Gospel of John) describes John the Baptist as 'a man sent from God' who 'was not the light' but 'came as a witness, to bear witness to the light, so that through him everyone might believe.' (John 1:6-8) Amer pointed to a hill in the middle-distance with a cave visible, he shared, 'That is where John the Baptist slept according to tradition.' It was not open to the public.

We then emerged from the forest into an open space and Amer told me this was the place. A small baptismal font had been built there and there were the remains of a church built there during the Byzantine era. The River only occasionally flows into this spot now during floods.

> *In those days, Jesus came from Nazareth of Galilee and was baptised by John in Jordan. When he came out of the water, immediately he saw the heavens being torn open and the Spirit descending on him like a dove. And a voice came from heaven, 'You are my beloved Son; with you I am well pleased.' – Mark 1:9-11*

It blew my mind to imagine them there then – these earth-shattering events which changed the world forever. We then walked on to the spot on the River where many baptisms were said to have taken place, and it was moving to see how moving it was to everyone gathered there (there were about ten tourists – weeping, laughing, hugging, praying). I took off my shoes and socks and bathed my feet in the River Jordan. Quite a moment in a life.

Madaba

We reached Madaba and Amer brought me into a room and picked up a long stick, stood in front of a large map on the wall and proceeded to tell me and a family who came in and joined us, about the creation and meaning of the map. The Byzantine floor mosaic (dating to the 6th century AD) contains the oldest surviving original cartographic depiction of the Holy Land and Jerusalem.

Amer points at a sign: (Just 5 mins to explain), "No chance", he laughed

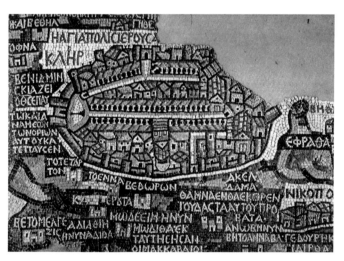

Jerusalem on the famous map

It truly was like something from a movie – an ancient map with pieces missing. I went into the church and marvelled at the mosaic masterpiece. Piece by piece, crafted and laid. A masterpiece.

After leaving the Church in Madaba, Amer asked if I was hungry. I very much was. Touring can be tiring! He brought me to a local restaurant in the town where his friend served us bowl after bowl of hummus and aubergines, chickpeas, falafel and pita, all bursting with zest, spice and flavour. The Jordanian hospitality and welcome was warm and genuine. Amer asked me what I wanted to drink – I said a Sprite – he bought me a local version – Jordan was boycotting Coca-Cola and other companies who were supporting the war in Gaza. When we were so full we couldn't eat any more, we got back on the road for the final part of the tour – Mt. Nebo.

Mt. Nebo

Our final stop of the day was Mt. Nebo. Moses is a figure venerated in all three Abrahamic religions. Why are they called Abrahamic? It was Abraham who first worshipped one God, who helped forge what became known as Monotheism. After fleeing slavery under the Pharaoh in Egypt, the Jewish people, the Israelites, lived in the desert for 40 years.

Amer spoke about the journey of Moses and his followers to this spot and the significance of finally glimpsing the Promised Land after centuries of slavery. Jewish tradition says that Moses died there having seen but not set foot in the Promised Land. Amer told me that in Islam it is believed that Moses went further and made it to Canaan.

The late Rev. Dr. Martin Luther King Jr. invoked the scene on Mount Nebo in the famous speech he delivered in Memphis the day before he was assassinated (1968). He said:

> 'Well, I don't know what will happen now. We've got some difficult days ahead. But it doesn't matter to me now. Because I've been to the mountaintop. And I don't mind. Like anybody, I would like to live a long life. Longevity has its place. But I'm not concerned about that now. I just want to do God's will. And He's allowed me to go up to the mountain. And I've looked over. And I've seen the promised land. I may not get there with you. But I want you to know tonight, that we, as a people, will get to the promised land.'
> 'I See the Promised Land,' April 3, 1968

Looking toward the Promised Land from Mt Nebo

The serpentine cross sculpture atop Mount Nebo was created by Italian artist Gian Paolo Fantoni. It is symbolic of the miracle of the bronze serpent invoked by Moses in the wilderness and the cross upon which Jesus was crucified. We stood and looked out over the Promised Land, promised by God to Jacob after he had wrestled the angel (who was really God) – symbolic of his struggle with his inner self to overcome deceit. Jacob was later renamed Israel – 'one who struggles for God' – and had 12 children, the twelve tribes of Israel. One of whom was Joseph (he of the technicolour Dreamcoat) who had settled in Egypt and had risen to wealth and status in Egyptian society.

Jacob travelled to Egypt to see Joseph before his death – God had told him that going there was the right thing to do and promised that his family would grow and prosper there, and that one day, his family would return to the Promised Land in Canaan. When famine struck Canaan, Jacob sent his sons to find help in Egypt, where they met Joseph and were saved from famine. However, in time the Egyptians resented their wealth and status and enslaved the Jewish people for hundreds of years before Moses (born a Jewish baby but raised by the Pharoah's sister after she found him in a basket) led them across the Red Sea and back as far as Mt. Nebo where he saw the Promised Land but never set foot there.

So much history, faith, progress and conflict over this place. To be reminded by Amer – in such vivid telling – of these biblical stories I had been told as a child and read about in the beautifully illustrated Children's Bible my Mum had given me for my Holy Communion... To stand there where Moses had stood here with his followers... So much of our shared human history and beliefs have developed from that time, from those stories – stories that connect the Jewish people, the

Muslim people and the Christian people – belief in One God – we are all sisters and brothers – connected. The enormity of it all.

I went into the chapel on the top of the hill which had been built upon the stonework, as well as around the mosaics from a Byzantine church built in 597 AD, which itself was built upon the foundations of earlier churches and tombs. The mosaics were mostly of trees and animals. Beautiful. Simple.

Mosaics in the chapel on Mt Nebo

The following morning, we hit the road at 9:30 AM, headed for Israel, which wasn't far away. On our journey, we passed a large factory outlet shop specialising in mud and beauty products, its sign flashing a tempting 50% off all items. We made a quick stop and Denis couldn't resist picking up a few purchases.

As we drove, we saw the sign for the Jordan River, the site where John the Baptist is said to have baptised Jesus. Interestingly, both Israel and Jordan claim the exact location within their borders, resulting in two competing sites for this significant historical event.

We finally reached the village near the border crossing and the scene was bustling with activity – taxis, carts, bags, trucks, vans, wheelie suitcases and overstuffed backpacks filled the area. Amidst the commotion, Amer skilfully guided us to the Jordanian departure building. After navigating through the necessary paperwork and paying the $15 departure tax, we secured cash for the shuttle bus to the crossing. We shared a heartfelt hug with Amer, grateful for his guidance and insights throughout our journey.

Reflecting on our time in Jordan, it's challenging to fully articulate our impressions and the people we encountered. Unlike our experiences in Syria, we didn't meet as many Jordanians. Perhaps it was due to the way we travelled, which felt more isolating. We weren't wandering through city streets or experiencing the everyday sights that come from being among locals. In many ways, we were just tourists, visiting renowned sites like Jerash, Petra, and the Dead Sea, all of which were stunning in their own right.

The service at the upscale hotels we stayed in was impeccable, delivered by well-trained staff, many of whom hailed from Asia. Yet, we didn't get a true sense of Jordanian culture beyond our interactions with Amer. He was nothing short of exceptional – a one-man show who blended the roles of storyteller, actor and historian. With a rare gift for simplifying thousands of years of history into engaging and insightful tales, he truly embodied the spirit of the 'brownies,' as he humorously referred to himself, of the Sham.

Thank you, Amer, for an unforgettable journey!

Amer our Jordanian guide: In his own words:

My name is Amer Nizami and I am a dedicated tourist guide based in the ancient city of Jerash, Jordan. While Jarash is where I call home and where my passion for history began, my guidance extends across the entire country of Jordan. This allows me to share the diverse and rich heritage of Jordanian history with visitors from all around the globe.

Growing up among the Roman ruins of Jerash inspired my career. The city's deep historical roots and architectural marvels fostered my love for guiding. The most rewarding part of my job is seeing my clients' satisfaction. Each tour is a unique experience, tailored to the varied interests and expectations of each visitor. I strive to balance their desires with the historical and cultural richness of Jordan, ensuring an enriching experience.

My family's history is deeply connected to the land. We are one of the earliest families to settle in modern Jerash. My grandfather was a significant figure, serving as the mayor in the 1930s and 1940s. Our family's legacy in Palestine and Jordan profoundly influences my guiding approach. My grandfather owned an olive farm in Palestine up until 1948 when it was taken by the occupation*. It is a personal mission for me to honour this heritage through my work, sharing the stories of both landscape and history.

Guiding across Jordan presents its own set of challenges. Each region has its unique characteristics and meeting the diverse needs of visitors while preserving the integrity of the sites requires careful balancing. Yet, it is this variety that makes my role so fulfilling. Each day offers a new opportunity to introduce visitors to the country's rich history, culture, and religious significance.

Ultimately, what drives me is the joy of contributing to a visitor's understanding and appreciation of Jordan. From the ancient ruins of Jerash to the stunning landscapes and historical sites throughout the country, I am honoured to guide and share the stories of this remarkable land – my home.' *Here, Amer is referring to events around the creation of the state of Israel.*

ISRAEL
State of Israel

לְאָרְשִׂי תַנִידְמ (Hebrew)

دَوْلَة إسْرائيل (Arabic)

AND
STATE OF PALESTINE
State of Palestine

دولة فلسطين (Arabic)

Dawlat Filasṭīn

Introduction to our friends the
Moshe and Tirza Hananel

When we first started planning our trip, long before the Gaza invasion, one of my main hopes was to visit Israel. Back in 1995, I spent a day in Eilat visiting friends – Moshe Hananel and his wife, Tirza. I've known Moshe for over 40 years. From the mid-1970s to the late 1980s, we worked together, helping to bring tourists from the USA to both Ireland and Israel. Those were tough years for international tourism, but by working closely with our American partners, we managed to make it work. Many of those connections are still friends today. A few years ago, Moshe and Tirza even visited Ireland and stayed with us. Despite our careers taking different paths, we remained in touch.

In September 2023, I reached out to Moshe and Tirza on Zoom to discuss our tentative plans. Given Moshe's deteriorating health – he has Parkinson's and Type 1 Diabetes – I wasn't sure he'd be up for visitors. But as we spoke, like old friends, Moshe was full of encouragement and touched by the idea that we still planned to visit. He has always been an incredibly positive person and over the next few weeks, we learned just how resilient he was – no obstacle, be it ill-health, culture, language, wars, or geopolitics, seemed insurmountable for him. *See Moshe postscript at the end.*

Then, in October 2023, Hamas attacked Israel, leaving thousands dead and hundreds taken hostage. Israel's response, and the horrific aftermath, are still unfolding as I write. Our plans, in comparison, felt so small in the face of such tragedy.

My son Denis was never entirely sure about visiting Israel, because of the conflict. He went along with it for my sake, knowing how much I wanted to see my friends, but also aware that I couldn't make the trip alone. I'm deeply grateful to him for accompanying me.

Moshe and I stayed in contact throughout December 2023 and into 2024, with ceasefire hopes being raised and dashed repeatedly. Our plans seemed to follow that same on-again, off-again rhythm. In the end, hoping for the best, we laid out a rough itinerary: Lebanon, Syria, Jordan, and, if possible, Israel. Moshe's advice was to visit Israel last, entering through Jordan at the Allenby Crossing, also known as the King Hussein Peace Bridge.

And so, the time had come.

We had said our goodbyes to Amer and found ourselves standing alone in the blazing midday sun in no-man's land between Jordan and Israel. Our first stop was a nearby building for the initial border check. We handed over our passports and paid Jordan's exit tax – everything was in order. Soon after, we boarded a bus that would take us to the Israeli border. It waited until it was full, with the last to board being an American family: a husband, wife, and their three children. As they passed our seats, the man asked where we were from and, when I told him, he mentioned that he had done Bible Studies in Belfast. What a small world! We quickly nicknamed him Pastor Bob. Dressed casually in a baseball cap and holiday shorts, Pastor Bob explained that his family lived in Jordan but were heading to Jerusalem for an important holiday weekend. At the time, the significance of the holiday didn't hit us but we later realised it was Orthodox Easter, taking place on Holy Saturday.

Once everyone was on board, a frontier official collected all our passports and disappeared with them while we remained seated. It was an uneasy wait and after what felt like an eternity, the official returned, handing back the passports one by one. The journey to the Israeli border continued for about 20 minutes, during which we passed hundreds of parked trucks, fully loaded but stationary. Later, we learned that most of these trucks were humanitarian aid vehicles destined for Gaza.

When we finally crossed the bridge and reached the Israeli border post, there were only around 30 to 40 people at the checkpoint, the majority of them Palestinians, with more women than men. We were guided into a well-air-conditioned building for the next round of security checks. Our bags, backpacks, and even my trusty walking pole went through two large screening machines as we queued for passport control, one step closer to our destination.

Denis and I were in separate queues, and while I knew his paperwork was in order, I noticed he was being questioned more thoroughly and eventually detained. It made sense – young, fit, and arriving in a country at war, his profile must have triggered a red flag.

Tirza & Moshe

I exited the building, and to my delight, there was my old friend Moshe, waiting for me with a shepherd's stick in hand. He was tall, though thinner and older than I remembered. Someone, after seeing a photo of him later, said, 'He looks like Abraham,' and they were right. Tirza soon joined us, and we hugged, relieved that we had made it across.

However, Denis was still inside, detained for questioning. Moshe explained that this was standard procedure – his details would be sent to Tel Aviv, and from there forwarded to Interpol, the CIA, and Dublin for verification. I grew anxious and stood on a nearby seat to peek over the partition to check if Denis was still there. I spotted him sitting calmly on a bench, reading a book. Immediately, three armed young officers approached me, sternly ordering me to get down. I did.

It was scorching outside, even in the shade, but Tirza, ever thoughtful, had prepared snacks – sliced apples and nuts, all neatly wrapped. We sat and waited while the border crossing remained relatively quiet, with little movement but plenty of uniformed soldiers and police officers bustling about. After three long hours, Denis finally emerged, calm and composed. After exchanging greetings, we were ready to hit the road.

Tirza took the wheel of their white 4x4, and we began our journey through the West Bank hills, east of Jerusalem. The landscape was barren, with few signs of habitation – just sheep and the occasional shepherd's shelter. Clearly, this was not a well-travelled road.

Along the way, we learned more about the border crossings between Jordan and Israel. There are two main international crossings – one in the north, near Amman, and the other in the south, between Aqaba and Eilat. Our crossing, the Allenby or King Hussein Bridge crossing, isn't a major international checkpoint but more of a convenience for workers, families, and truck drivers. Notably, visas cannot be issued here, and Israeli citizens are not permitted to use it unless they're on a pilgrimage to Mecca, for which they must have a Jordanian visa in advance.

With the formalities behind us, we finally made our way toward Jerusalem.

Denis's Thoughts On Entering Israel

Dad sailed through but I was asked to wait. I was not told for what or for who or why or how long. So I sat down beside a man with long hair and a pleasant face and gentle voice. He turned out to be Dan from California who was living in Tijuana, the Mexican city immediately inside the border with the United States and San Diego. He said he is an activist who manages a garden on both sides of the wall separating the two countries. He said that the garden had been destroyed on the US side which he found heart-breaking, but they have started again, nature connecting both sides.

I asked him how much of the wall had now been built, he said approximately 700 miles. I asked him if he had any ideas for how the immigration situation could be better managed. He said that there had to be a more humanitarian way of dealing with migrants rather than locking them in open-air holding cells and separating children from parents. He spoke about the different ways people try to get across the border – in trucks, using ladders, paying huge amounts to human traffickers. He was in the Middle East learning Arabic. He seemed like a really kind soul.

Suddenly, the unsmiling man with big biceps (a less obviously kind soul) who seemed to be in charge of deciding whether we were allowed into Israel or not emerged from a room with glass mirrors and gave him the green light. Dan and I said our goodbyes. It was just me now.

Many more minutes passed but no one came. I asked the man at the desk, he said it might take some time. I wondered if they were searching my social media history – I had posted about a demonstration I had attended in Dublin in February 2024 in support of a Palestinian State.

Biceps man finally returned and gave me a form to fill out about where I had been before visiting Israel. I asked him why it was taking so long for me to go through. He said they were investigating my connection with Syria after my recent visit. I responded with barely disguised impatience (having had no food or water or coffee for what felt like an age), 'is that what the delay is? We were there for tourism, you could have just asked me instead of leaving me sitting here for over two hours with my Dad and his friends outside.' He said harshly – 'if you argue with us it will take much longer.' I swiftly recognized it would be daft to debate with him and muttered meekly – 'yes, no problem, I'll fill this form out now – is there anywhere I can get coffee and water please?'

It turned out there was a kiosk I could go to around the corner for water and coffee. After handing the form back to him, another hour drifted by, before he emerged and gave me the clearance I needed to enter Israel.

I walked out into the hot afternoon sun and met Moshe and Tirza and apologised for keeping them for so long. Tirza gave me sandwiches and fruit and dates and we chatted in the car and I revived. The next leg of our adventure had begun and who knew what lay ahead? Should we even have been there? Dad wanted to meet his great friend Moshe though, and I wanted him to have a chance to do this and to see The Holy Land.

Before leaving Ireland, and as we had travelled around Lebanon, Syria and Jordan, I had been very uncertain about spending a large amount of time in the company of Israeli people (who I had never met) given my feelings (and the horror of many people I had met along the way) about what was happening in Gaza. I was also deeply disturbed the more I learned about the system of apartheid and forced occupation that had been implemented for decades since the Nakba (which is Arabic for catastrophe) – the ethnic cleansing of Palestinian Arabs to create room for Jews to populate the land that became Israel. I was worried we would be given a one-sided view of the situation from our Israeli hosts.

This was the Nakba, according to Wikipedia.

> 'In the 1948 Palestine war, more than 750,000 Palestinian Arabs – about half of Mandatory Palestine's predominantly Arab population – were expelled or fled from their homes, at first by Zionist paramilitaries, and after the establishment of Israel, by its military.
>
> The expulsion and flight was a central component of the fracturing, dispossession, and displacement of Palestinian society, known as the Nakba. Dozens of massacres targeting Arabs were conducted by Israeli military forces and between 400 and 600 Palestinian villages were destroyed. Fifteen thousand arabs were murdered. Village wells were

poisoned in a biological warfare programme codenamed Operation Cast Thy Bread and properties were looted to prevent Palestinian refugees from returning. Other sites were subject to Hebraization of Palestinian place names.'

Both Dad and I had a done a fair bit of reading about the history of the region, and while it made sense to me that the Jewish people needed and deserved a state of their own where they could be free from persecution (especially after The Holocaust), the way that it had happened left the entire enterprise tarnished from the very start. Could an Israeli state have been achieved differently? That question would take a long time to analyse and answer. The foundation of the state of Israel was either an inspirational bid for survival by a people who had nearly been exterminated with the slaughter by the Nazis of six million of their brothers and sisters or else it was a brutal land grab resulting in the displacement of 750,000 Arab Palestinians and the deaths of 15,000 people. Can two things be true at the same time depending on perspective?

From my own reading, it was clear that Jewish people have contributed more to modern human prosperity and to scientific and creative progress per head of population than any other people on Earth (similar to the achievements of The Islamic Golden Age) – especially when viewed through the prism of Nobel Prizes:

Of the 965 recipients of the Nobel Prize and the Nobel Memorial Prize in Economic Sciences between 1901 and 2023, at least 216 have been Jews or people with at least one Jewish parent, representing 22 per cent of all recipients. Yet Jews comprise only 0.2% of the world's population, meaning their share of winners is 110 times their proportion of the world's population.

‘The Mystery of Jewish Nobel Prize Laureates’. Jewish Nobel Prize Winners. ANU – Museum of the Jewish People. Retrieved 6 October 2023.

However, it seemed to me that the Jewish ultra-Orthodox views about the God-given right of their people to more and more land at the expense of the Palestinian people was the opposite of Godly. But I wanted to be open-minded and get to know

Dad's friends without any presumptions as to how they may think or feel. The attacks of October 7th were so despicable, cutting down the lives of so many innocent people. It was clear the entire nation of Israel was emotionally scarred and were living through a nightmare as they pleaded, prayed and wished for the safe return of the 200+ hostages – to many their friends, neighbours, colleagues, relatives and loved ones.

Dermod & Moshe

Kids playing in Jerusalem

Israel Day 1

Arrival – Pontifical Institute Notre Dame of Jerusalem and Sherover Theatre

We arrived with no advance planning, no hotels booked, no itinerary and no schedules. Our friends had arranged everything.

Over the next week we travelled the entire country. We went to Tel Aviv on the Mediterranean coast in central Israel, to the Erez border crossing into Gaza in southern Israel, and to the north, to the Sea of Galilee nestling against the Golan Heights. While Israel was a country at war, we came across no checkpoints or signs of military movements. It was business as usual. But there were no tourists at all – the only exception being a scattering of religious tourists in Jerusalem for the Orthodox Easter. Our hosts wanted to ensure we experienced an open, unbiased visit to Israel. They arranged separate guides for two different days. A Jewish Israeli guide for one day and a Palestinian Guide for another.

Before arriving in Israel, we had already completed two weeks of an incredible, once in a lifetime trip. Now we were in a country at war. Somehow, I expected to see loads of military, checkpoints and disruption. I presumed we would find a locked down, darkened and subdued Jerusalem. But as we drove into the city, the evening traffic was bustling and the light rail trains and buses were full of commuters going home. Massive road works were in hand as extra motorways were under construction.

We arrived at what would be our hotel and Tirza announced, 'We have booked you into a very special place. I hope you will like it.' We stopped at a security gatehouse and spoke to the guard. He indicated where to go and we drove in and circled in front of the main pillared entrance. We saw before us a massive, majestic granite building on a hill overlooking the city directly opposite the New Gate – the Old City of Jerusalem. Our bags were unloaded into an air-conditioned lobby. We were staying in the Vatican owned Pontifical Institute Notre Dame of Jerusalem Centre, a 120 bedroomed guesthouse/hotel for pilgrims, popes and cardinals! And naturally, my room was fit for those only ordained to wear purple. The porter brought us up to our third-floor rooms. But Moshe and Tirza wanted to inspect them as well. They were huge rooms with high ceilings, some tasteful wall surrounds and windows overlooking the Old City. A small crucifix was positioned over each bed.

We thought our hosts might now feel they had their duty done for the day, but not so. 'We will meet you down in the lobby in twenty minutes,' they said and so began one of the most whirlwind, non-stop weeks of my life. Moshe and Tirza are like a pair of Duracell bunnies – they didn't want us to waste a moment or miss an experience during our time with them. Soon we were back in the car and heading to Sherover Theatre for a performance of the Jerusalem Symphony Orchestra described as – *'A Salute to the Young Soloists of Jerusalem: A concert with young soloists under the baton of Guy Feder'.*

The Jerusalem Symphony Orchestra was founded in 1936 by the Palestine Broadcasting Service and in 1948 became an integral part of the Israeli Broadcasting Association. On their website, they recognise themselves as 'a cultural champion of peace and reconciliation.' As we stepped into the Sherover Theatre, we took some time to explore the expansive foyer. It was home to a striking modern art exhibition, with powerful pieces that delved into the harsh realities of war. What an introduction to Israel. We enjoyed two magical hours of every genre of music, song and dance.

Back in the car, it was finally time to eat. Tirza drove us to a lively shopping street lined with upscale brands, trendy shops, and bustling cafes, all brightly lit and inviting. The streets were filled with people casually strolling, shopping and dining, creating a vibrant and relaxed atmosphere. We found a cosy restaurant and settled in for a much-needed meal.

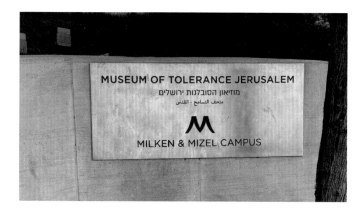

On the way back, we passed a small pro-war encampment – surprisingly, the only one we encountered during all our travels around the country. Once back at the hotel, I called home to share the day's events. What had struck us most was the unexpected sense of normality in such uncertain times.

Denis's thoughts:

Moshe and Tirza were such incredibly nice people. I relaxed into their company, seeing them as people, as individuals, and my preconceptions evaporated.. After a lovely pizza and a beer, they brought us to see a performance of students from the college of music performing with the symphony orchestra.

Some of the pieces were achingly beautiful. I sat watching the performance, my mind oscillating between the magic of the music and the incongruity of the situation. I found it jarring beyond words to listen to such beautiful music at the Concert Hall while such indiscriminate atrocities were being carried out not far from here. My mind felt bifurcated. The walls of the building were decorated with children's art made since October 7th as their response to the trauma – tears and hope, and peace and love. So simple, so moving... and yet nothing about this situation is or was or can be simple. It struck me that Israeli/Palestinian people could only see a certain amount, and maybe that goes for all people – we believe what we need to believe in order to keep going, keep living. And filter out the rest.

Some of the art on the walls of the Concert Hall was moving, but all telling of their side, their experience. I needed to see an understanding beyond themselves, the bigger picture. If God exists, God loves all their children. On the one hand, I thought – how could these people be here at this concert, just getting on with life? But then I thought – what else could they be doing? I guess they were not the ones who chose war, or whose choices led others to choose terror.

I really liked our hosts, but I also wanted some mind space to explore and experience things for myself. I asked them if it would be possible for me to visit the West Bank during my time there. They understood, and although they had their concerns, they said they would see what they could do. And they very kindly organised for their friend, Ibrahim, to take me around for the day. Any presumption I had had about them – that they may be close-minded or unable to see the world through our eyes – had disappeared. Moshe, with his decades of experience in tourism, chose both Martin and Ibrahim as our guides around Jerusalem and The West Bank precisely because they were independent thinkers.

Denis with Moshe & Tirza

Night view of the Old City

Israel Day 2 – Jerusalem

East Jerusalem, The Chapel of the Ascension, Garden of Gethsemane, Tour of Old City and Church of the Holy Sepulchre

Bright and early the next morning, we were picked up by our Israeli guide, Martin Goldberg, who arrived in his SUV. Martin, an experienced guide based in Israel, specialises in tours around Jerusalem and its surrounding areas. Originally from England, he moved to Israel with his parents in 1982. Stocky and fit, with the unmistakable remnants of a Manchester accent, Martin is a former member of the Israeli army. Beyond his work as a guide, he dedicates his time to a special volunteer group that protects West Bank Palestinians from harassment or displacement by illegal Jewish settlers.

Martin telling Denis about Jerusalem

Moshe & Martin

*Martin's Israeli friend at
an anti-governnment protest*

Martin Goldberg – Israeli Guide And Activist Helping Palestinian Farmers

My name is Martin Goldberg and I popped into this world sixty years ago. I was brought up in an observant Jewish family in London. I remember joking with my parents at holiday times that planes land all over the world, not just in Tel Aviv but suffice to say we visited Israel a great deal. After taking my A levels I came to Israel for a gap year and have been here ever since. The best way to describe my relationship with this country is a love/hate one. Generally, I love to hate it but it still is my home and I will fight and do everything in my power to make my home a better place. I will fight for equality for all its citizens, for a separation of religion from State and for rights for the Palestinian People.

I used to work as a professional tour guide but I returned my licence because I felt I could not guide in good faith with the right-wing government policies that I find abhorrent. My time is filled with activism, the main item being defending Palestinian shepherding communities in the Jordan valley. These communities are the most underprivileged in Palestine and are the target of daily attacks from Messianic settlers, aided by the Israeli army and police force.

In the communities we try to protect, we have a 24/7 presence, placing ourselves between the attackers and the Palestinians. I have been injured on more than one occasion but giving up is not an option. Since the barbaric attack on October 7th, 24 different shepherding communities have been forcibly displaced from their lands and have been forced to live in squalid conditions elsewhere, the reason behind all this, is ethnic cleansing of the area. It is important that people in the world know that there are some (not a lot) of Israelis that drive hundreds of kms a day to put their bodies on the line for doing what's right and of course all the volunteers do not get paid a cent and fund the activity out of their own pocket.

Denis's thoughts on Martin:

As we were eating breakfast, a man in his late 50s/early 60s came up and introduced himself asking if we were Dermod and Denis. We were, we said. His name was Martin Goldberg. He told us we had two reasons not to like him – one he was British, and two he was Israeli.

He was good-natured and good-humoured, and I relaxed into his knowledge and his company. He had moved from Britain to Israel in 1980, full of idealistic hope for a shared socialist future. After living in a Kibbutz for a year, he had then worked for the army on special operations to deal with people who were a barrier to peace negotiations. He would no longer work as a tour guide because he didn't want to be told what he could and couldn't say by the government. He had taken Tony Blair and other senior politicians and diplomats on tours, and felt he was being leant on to only give one version of events. Now he worked with an organisation helping to prevent Palestinian farmers from having their land taken from them by armed Israeli settlers. The previous week he said he had been attacked by his countrymen, and sliced with a knife along his thigh before being put in prison. He had no self-pity, and clearly had found some comfort in following his conscience.

We had the most extraordinary day with him as Dad has described. I had been in Jerusalem once before – with its sacred sights and bustling stalls – and it was very special to be there with Dad.

Jerusalem – the place that has touched humanity more than any other – for better and for worse.

In front of the golden dome of the Temple on the Mount, also known as the al-Aqsa Mosque, one of the holiest sites in Islam.

View of the Old City from Mount of Olives

Martin explained to us that we would start outside the city walls, up in the hills overlooking the city. We drove up narrow residential streets and eventually found ourselves high in an area near the Mount of Olives overlooking the city. We were in East Jerusalem.

We began the day with a visit to the Chapel of the Ascension which we were told is under the control of the Palestinians in East Jerusalem. We passed through an archway into a gravel courtyard and a small stone building. We were taken back by the simplicity of the site and the single stone slab believed to be marked with a footprint of Jesus as he ascended into heaven.

Outside, crossing the road we looked across a valley at the walls of the city, the Dome of the Rock was golden and shimmering in the sun. The Dome is the site of the Al-Aqsa mosque and is one of Islam's three holiest sites (the others being Mecca and Medina, both in Saudi Arabia). Below us we could see The Jewish Cemetery – Martin explained that the Jewish Cemetery on the Mount of Olives is the oldest and most important Jewish cemetery in Jerusalem. The Mount of Olives has been a traditional Hebrew/Jewish burial location since antiquity. It holds thousands of tombs. Apart from the ones entitled to be buried there – Rabbis and Scholars and Hasidic Rebbes, the Mount of Olives is every Jew's dream for their final resting place. For the few that can afford it, it is still possible but very expensive to get a plot. Jewish tradition has it that when the Messiah returns, the Day of the Resurrection of the dead will begin here.

Back in the car and down narrow streets, we arrived at the side entrance to the Garden of Gethsemane. We had this wonderful, serene garden all to ourselves and really enjoyed walking in the shade of the trees, following narrow paths with flowering bougainvillaea all around. On the left was a small grotto/chapel with the large half circle window behind the altar framing Jerusalem. Nearby is the site of the Tomb of the Virgin Mary, where the mother of Jesus is believed to have been buried.

Parallel to the outer road is the Church of All Nations (The Basilica of the Agony) built around the rock where Jesus prayed the night before his crucifixion. The church designed by the famous Italian architect, Antonio Barluzzi, was built in 1924 by donations from many nations of the world (hence the name) The gardens, grotto and church are maintained now by the Franciscan Order. We were the only visitors there that day. As we sat in the shade of the Basilica doors listening to Martin, a veiled Palestinian woman passed with her daily shopping. We were reminded that this is a living community.

Church of All Nations (Garden of Gethsemanae)

We returned to the New Gate to join the walking tour of the Old City. We went down through myriads of narrow alleyways and streets until we emerged into an open area historically called the Wailing Wall or in Islam, called the Buraq Wall, and then to the large section used for Jewish prayer, which is called the Western Wall.

The scene at this Wall is almost indescribable. There is a large open area in front of it, a paved square in effect. Many people will be familiar with this site as it often features on the world media – sadly, for the wrong reasons. It is a place of veneration but also of conflict. One side of the wall is part of the retaining structure of the Temple Mount. Temple Mount is the holiest place where Jews are permitted to pray but entry to it is very restricted. The outside wall provides the nearest devotees can get to the holy of holies. The sun was blazing, there were no tourists but hundreds of Orthodox and Hasidic Jews, all men, young and old filling the area. They were dressed in their daily black garb, wide black hats, white shirts with white tassels, and all sporting the very distinctive hairstyle called *payos*, which are long ringlets usually in front of each ear. The area, despite its religious aura, was frantic with activity and fervour. Men guided you towards the wall and if your head was bare, you were offered a kippah or yarmulke (white skullcap) to respectfully cover the top of your head.

At the Western Wall

We wrote individual wishes, stuffed the papers in crevices in the wall and prayed standing up like all the others. The practice of placing prayer notes in the Wall has been traced to the Midrashic teaching that the Divine Presence has never moved from the Western Wall. Also the Kabbalistic teaching that all prayers ascend to Heaven through the Temple Mount, which the Western Wall abuts. Martin said that this area would normally be jammed with long queues and priority given to Hasidic students. For an area that could probably accommodate thousands and thousands – it was almost empty.

Next on our itinerary was a tour of the tunnels beneath the Western Wall. As we waited in the ticket office with about 20 other people, we were pleasantly surprised to see a familiar face – none other than Pastor Bob and his family! Imagine our delight as they joined the group.

The Hidden Passageway runs from east to west and is believed to have been the route King David used to travel from the Jaffa Gate to the Temple Mount, to pray. Close by is the Great Bridge where the Priests of Jerusalem ('Kohanim', descendants of the Sons of Aaron) walked. According to the Western Wall tunnels guidebook:

> *'The Western Wall (the Kotel in Hebrew) is impressive, but its greatness is truly discovered when you descend underground to the Western Wall Tunnels. The tunnels run along approximately 488 metres of the Western Wall. These complex underground tunnels create a direct link between the history of the Hasmonean period and modern times. The tunnels are supported by many arches and contain*

stairways that connected the ancient city with the Temple Mount, over the Tyropoeon Valley that ran along the western side of the Temple Mount, separating the two. Today these passageways support streets and homes in the Muslim Quarter. The tunnels were first discovered during digs done by British archaeologists in the 19th century, but the real digging was done after the Six Day War, after 1967, by the Israeli Ministry of Religions.'

Emerging into the daylight on a totally different street from where we entered, we realised that the city is like a jigsaw and a web of routes and diminutive streets. The Old City is traffic free with only deliveries and disabled vehicles permitted. There are no car parks. Apparently, the only road that enters is through the Jaffa Gate and leaves through the Dung Gate.

Ho ho Holy Land

When speaking of the Jaffa Gate to Moshe, he mentioned in passing that somebody had sold the rights to the trade name Jaffa. It is now used as the Brand name globally for oranges – none of which originate in Israel!

Dermod & Martin

Back into the maze of alleyways and sloping streets, shopping souks with crowds of people, with the main products, religious icons. The vendors do what market vendors do, calling out and inviting the passersby to stop. In such circumstances, I usually avoid eye contact and speed up. As I hurried along I could hear the click-clack of my walking stick on the cobbles. I was aware of one of the shop vendors keeping up the pace with me. I sped up. He followed me, then opened his hand and showed me a piece of black rubber. He gestured, 'Come back, come back, you need this.' I retraced my steps to his shop and thankfully bought the metal reinforced heavy-duty sheath for the steel tip of my walking pole. It cost $5. My travel companions and I were very grateful to him.

A craftsman's workshop

Next was a visit to the House of Caiaphas, where Jesus was brought to trial before being passed on to Pontius Pilate. The House of Caiaphas is also associated with Peter's denial of Jesus, three times before the cock crowed. Climbing some steps we happened upon a large crowd of men, women and children all dressed and draped in white. In an open courtyard, several hundred were all excited, chattering and eating. Denis joined them while Martin and I watched. He was offered a plate of Doro Wat. (He knew this dish of chicken stew from his trip to Ethiopia in 2008.) They were all pilgrims from Ethiopia, there for the feast day.

Martin led us to the Church of the Holy Sepulchre which is built on the traditional site of where Jesus was crucified and buried. This is not at all a great imposing building standing aloft on a hill. It is somewhat understated and hidden away built into a hill of the city. Arriving at the small square at the entrance we found it was a hive of activity. There were large screens being erected, TV and other broadcast cables everywhere, technicians all over the place; all preparing for the next day's celebration of Holy Saturday when Orthodox Christians celebrated the burial and resurrection of Christ.

Aedicule containing the tomb of Jesus

Our visit to the Church of the Holy Sepulchre was special in many ways and we were very moved by it. Stepping in from the bright sunlight, we climbed up a relatively small stairway to reach a heavily adorned altar. We followed the ritual of those before us and, taking our turn, we stooped down under the altar to kiss the stone on which, it is believed, stood the cross upon which Jesus was crucified. People around us were visibly very emotional. It was clearly a sacred space for Christian pilgrims. There was a respectful sombreness in the air. Then we went down another stair to the stone where Jesus's body was laid out and then to the Holy of Holies itself, the small church where Jesus was buried. Only three people at a time are allowed to enter this hallowed space. Again, everyone kissed the stone covering the tomb.

Prior to the October 2023 Hamas massacres, when the region was peaceful, religious tourism was normal. If we had visited then, we would have had to queue for many hours at each of the places we intimately experienced during less than a half a day.

Site of Jesus' crucifixion (Church of the Holy Sepulchre)

One of the extraordinary features about the whole region within what we call the Holy Land is the number of faiths that claim many of the historic places as sacred to their beliefs. For this reason, many of the religious sites are contested. The overlapping claims stem from the shared Abrahamic heritage, yet due to the intensity of feelings around these areas there is also much conflict. The conflicts seem to arise because control of these sites is intertwined with national identity and historical grievances. In the case of the Church of the Holy Sepulchre, we read that:

> 'The Status Quo, an understanding between religious communities dating to 1757, applies to the site. Control of the church itself is shared among several Christian denominations and secular entities in complicated arrangements essentially unchanged for over 160 years, and some for much longer. The main denominations sharing property over parts of the church are the Roman Catholic, Greek Orthodox, Armenian Apostolic, Coptic, Syriac, and Ethiopian Orthodox churches.'

The final twist is that the keys to the Church of the Holy Sepulchre are retained by a Muslim family.

A priest plays the piano

Jerusalem streetscape

Three Missionary of Charity Nuns in Jerusalem

We walked back up the streets out through the New Gate across the road to our hotel and said our goodbyes to Martin. He was a tremendous guide – practical, honest, nuanced and an expert on all faiths, including every Christian, Jewish and Islam shrine in this very special city. He openly disagrees with the current government military stance and war in Gaza. He and other ex-military colleagues work in the Israeli-occupied West Bank, trying to protect Palestinians from attack by Jewish settlers.

Sound & Light at the Citadel

An hour later Tirza and Moshe arrived to collect us to take us to our next event. The Night Spectacular – at the Tower of David Museum – Sound and Light at the Citadel. And spectacular it is. It opens to thundering music and the surrounding walls lighting up with imagery. A moving tableau of pictures tells the story of the city from its earliest times as a centre of trade and crafts and as a place of battle between various conquerors and empires – Egyptians, Crusaders and Ottomans. The music, the sounds of horses' hooves, of craft making, of fashion, of children playing, of destruction and rebuilding and of singing envelopes the audience and the castle. Special parking permits are very helpful as Moshe's disablement status is permitted by the special door to our parked car.

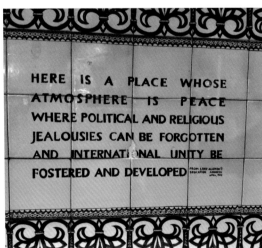

YMCA Jerusalem

Never without surprises, Moshe had more in mind – off to see the YMCA. This was the renowned Officers Club built by and for the British during their thirty-year, 1917–1948, administrative rule of Palestine. It has a floodlight edifice, a central tower, a courtyard, swimming pool and a five-star former officers' mess. Part of the building now houses a large children's crèche, run, we are told, by a Palestinian lady.

Directly across the road is the most legendary hotel of the region – the King David Hotel built in 1931. This five star, eight storey hotel views the Old City and Mount Zion. It continues to play host to visiting heads of state and distinguished guests. The hotel has been the scene for many historic and occasional tragic events. On 22nd of July 1946, Irgun terrorist Zionist fighters blew up the southern wing of the hotel containing offices for the British authorities, killing over 90 people including civilians.

As a former hotelier myself, I was pleased to visit the King David Hotel. It was impressive in every sense – subdued and dated. Passing security, we walked by the reception and concierge areas into a high ceiling but low-lit lobby featuring different seating areas. Down the centre was a marble walkway with the signatures of many of its famous guests inscribed – King Hussein, US Presidents Nixon, Ford, Carter, Clinton, George W Bush, Obama, Trump and Biden. Other heads of state and notables included King Charles, Churchill and Blair. Also Thatcher, Modi, Major, Kissinger, Elizabeth Taylor, Richard Gere and even Madonna.

Tirza drew my attention to several young couples on couches in the hotel lobby. Each pair intently sitting upright at right angles to each other. She told me in a low voice, 'These are arranged dates for young Orthodox or Hasidic couples.' I wandered around trying not to be a curious onlooker. The young men in their hats, white shirts with tassel trimmings, black suits and black shoes and the young women, intent and very serious looking, wearing white blouses, dark skirts and sensible shoes. Their hair was tidy and they wore no adornments at all. They all seemed to be wearing thick glasses. No sign of a smile or a grin.

Hasidic and Ultra-Orthodox Jews represent a large segment of the Jewish population of Israel. Normally right wing, currently they hold the balance of power. At the same time, they refuse to serve in the army. Although while we were in Israel, the Knesset passed the first reading of a new law to require all to serve in the army.

What is the Hasidic way of life? What are Hasidic traditions?

In the ultra-Orthodox Jewish community, potential partners often meet through matchmakers, with dates arranged under the guidance of both families. This tradition, deeply rooted in Jewish law, ensures that the process of finding a spouse is thoughtful and deliberate. The Talmud emphasises that a man must meet and find favour with a woman before marriage and a woman must be mature enough to make an informed decision about her potential husband. Both must fully consent and feel comfortable with the match.

Dating in this context is serious and purposeful, not intended for casual relationships or entertainment. It is reserved for mature individuals who are actively seeking a life partner, with the ultimate goal of creating a stable and compatible marriage. These restrictions are not about old-fashioned prudishness but rather focus on building strong, enduring unions.

In Hasidic tradition, the mitzvot – commandments – govern every aspect of life, from acts of charity and dietary laws to observing the Sabbath and studying the Torah. Hasidic communities, known as courts, are closely knit and revolve around a dynastic leader called the Rebbe. The Rebbe holds both spiritual and political authority within the community.

On significant occasions such as the Sabbath and holidays, the Rebbe hosts a Tisch (meaning table), a grand feast for his male followers. During this event, attendees sing, dance, and share meals while the Rebbe blesses his followers and delivers sermons. For Hasidim, even everyday actions are seen as sacred, embodying the ideal of living a life fully devoted to spiritual purpose and connection with God. – Perplexity

Hasidic Jews gather in Jerusalem

We left and yes there was yet another stop. It was past 11 PM and all we had managed since the afternoon was a quick falafel, eaten on the go in the Old City. Tirza had an idea: 'Let's head to the Turkish Railway station,' she said and off we went.

We pulled up right at the entrance of what turned out to be a stunning transformation of a historical site. The station dates back to 1892 and was part of the first railway line in the Middle East. Originally a narrow-gauge railway, it had served the French and Ottomans post-World War I before it was closed in 1948. It reopened a year later under Israel Railways but now the tracks are no longer in use. Instead, the buildings have found new life, housing a selection of restaurants and bars, turning the space into a lively gathering spot. The vibe was energetic, and we soon found a charming spot to enjoy our long-awaited meal.

The Turkish Railway Station

As we left, a large mural on a wall across from our car caught our attention. Stark and powerful, it displayed images of those who had been kidnapped by Hamas on October 7ᵗʰ and were still missing. With dark backgrounds and vivid red borders and hearts, the mural was a haunting reminder of those taken seven months ago. The simple hashtag, *#BringThemHomeNow,* echoed the ongoing pain and uncertainty that lingered in the air.

Day 3: Jerusalem/Ein Karem/ Mevaseret Zion

Early next morning I awake to the sound of my phone buzzing. A message from Moshe read, 'Holocaust Martyrs and Heroes Remembrance Day 2024 will be on Monday, May 6th. The State Opening Ceremony will be held at Yad Vashem on Sunday, May 5th at 20:00. We are invited to attend and so are you.'

We knew from recent chats with people that this is the key annual Holocaust remembrance event in Israel and we were now invited guests. That was an honour we could not pass. Denis and I talked and decided that we would definitely extend our time in Jerusalem to attend this ceremony. Our schedule for Israel was, inevitably, always flexible and open to adjustments. The hotel extended our stay for two extra nights without any issues.

After breakfast Moshe and Tirza arrived to pick us up with the news that the L.S Mayer Institute of Islamic Art would open early to facilitate our visit. We drove a short distance to the museum. From their literature, we read that:

> 'The L.S. Mayer Museum for Islamic Art was founded and funded by Vera Salomons, the scion of an aristocratic Anglo-Jewish family of enlightened activists in the cause of justice and civil rights. The museum of Islamic Art strives to realise the dream of Vera Salomons and honour her family legacy as being a bridge between Arab and Jewish cultures. It sees cultivation of cultural dialogue as its primary goal.'

A map of food & trade routes

Dermod with the Marie Antoinette watch created by Abraham-Louis Breguet

An artefact donated by Moshe & Tirza

The director, Dr Gilad Levian, is a friend of Moshe's and graciously brings us on a private tour of the museum. We were taken first to the Sir David Salomons Collections of Watches and Clocks. Sir David was Vera's father. It is hard to do justice to the display. We were presented with a room full of glittering glass cases beautifully displaying priceless time pieces through the ages. The central highlight piece is the 800-piece watch, named the Breguet Grande Complication, made for Marie Antoinette in 1783. It was once described as The Mona Lisa of timepieces. In 2013, it was valued at $30 million USD. Therein lies a tale of a heist and more:

> It [the Marie Antoinette watch] was stolen from the L.S. Mayer Institute for Islamic Art on April 17, 1983, along with more than 100 other rare timepieces from Salomons' collection. The theft was unsolved for 23 years until the police were tipped off by people who reported to have been shown pieces from the collection. It turned out that master-thief Na'aman Diller had committed the theft, hiding the watches in safes in the United States, Europe and Israel. After Diller's death, his widow tried to sell the stolen watches and clocks in 2004. She was caught and given 5 years' probation for accepting stolen goods. Of the 106 timepieces that were stolen, only 39 were recovered in 2007, including the Marie Antoinette. The watches were returned to the museum in Jerusalem.'

The collection was truly breathtaking, and the director shared his hopes of one day taking it on tour. After exploring the exhibit, we headed upstairs to the main attraction – a thematic exhibition tracing the history of Islamic cuisine through the ages. One display that particularly caught my attention was a section dedicated to the evolution of table manners

Various rules of etiquette for communal meals evolved from eating traditions attributed to the Prophet Mohammad. Emphasis was placed on using only three fingers of the right hand, maintaining clean hands, and waiting for others before taking food. At the Abbasid court in the eighth and ninth centuries, a body of literature on table manners emerged within the Arab genre, offering satirical depictions of stereotypical diners as a way to educate on proper behaviour.

Next to this display were playful cartoon illustrations of these dining *types*, including characters like Mr Cow, The Flusher, The Roudslicer, The Laryngealistor, The Foulmouth, The Pickpocket, Mr Camel and The Devourer.

Moving on to the section of the museum devoted to the Hajj:

> *The Hajj is the pilgrimage to Mecca and its surrounding holy sites and is one of the five basic commandments that must be observed by every able-bodied and able-minded adult Muslim – man and woman. The custom of making a pilgrimage to the shrines in and outside of Mecca in the spring and the winter existed even prior to Islam's founding. Muhammad revived this ancient, monotheistic, Arab ritual and inventively integrated it into Islam. He associated the founding of the kaaba with Abraham and his son Ishmael, therefore intending it for the worship of one God.*
>
> *The kaaba is a square, 15-metre-high building with no windows and only one door and is covered by a black cloth embroidered with a passage from the Quran. Its eastern wall houses a black stone, believed by some to be a meteor, with a diameter of approximately 30 cm.*

According to tradition, the stone was white but gradually became black from the sins of the people who touched it.

The Muslim must observe the commandment out of purity and sanctity, bare-headed and barefoot, wearing a special garment made from two unsewn white sheets. For the duration of the pilgrimage, he is forbidden to cut his hair and fingernails, to shave, to engage in marital relations and to spill blood.

Stepping out of the museum and into the daylight, our next destination took us beyond the city limits. We were headed to a unique midday opera performance, held in a private home with a cosy stage and studio attached – a truly intimate setting for such an experience. We went to The Eden-Tamir Centre, in the village of Ein Karem set in a valley surrounded by streams and trees. It was an extraordinary setting for The Singers of Meitar Opera Studio of the Israel Opera.

A front row seat for the Opera singers

We were treated to an hour and a half of exquisite oral interpretations, arias and duets from the famous operas of Mozart, Dvorak, Gluck, Puccini and more. The singers are attached to the studio which acts as an experimental incubator for existing and upcoming members of the Israel Opera Company. Opera connecting to an open-air setting was a new experience for me – the air was gentle with a slight breeze fanning all the smells and rustlings from the garden outside.

When it was over we left the car parked in the garden shade and walked a couple of hundred metres to the small village for lunch. On the way there, Tirza showed us the small grotto and well from which the Virgin Mary is said to have drunk. Ein Karem is the village where, as described in the New Testament, Mary visited her cousin, Elizabeth, when they were both pregnant – Mary with Jesus and Elizabeth with John the Baptist. Further up the hill we visited the church dedicated to Mary and Elizabeth. No pilgrims, no visitors – just scaffolding, as the interior is under restoration.

After lunch, in the shade, in a busy local café, Tirza announced, 'We are taking you to our home now.' A short drive up the hill and soon we arrive in a small housing enclave on the top of a hill. Their home is detached and on its own plot, beside a small park with extensive views from the roof terrace. 'We have lived here since we married. We never moved,' they explained. The lovely mature garden is testament to years of care and nurturing. We welcomed the coolness indoors. Their beautiful home is packed full of mementos of their lives from art, rugs, vases, porcelain, icons, statues, swords, scimitars, masks, collections of prayer beads, carvings, clocks, books and magazines – all special and meaningful. There is only one way to describe it – it is a veritable Aladdin's Cave. In the living room, on the low coffee table, they had put together a collection to show and tell us. The collection included:

- Historical maps – showing the various proposals for carving up Palestine and nearby countries.

- The G.A. Cohen clock and chandeliers which were given as a wedding present to Tirza by the granddaughter of Margarethe Cohen Micheels and Emanuel Micheels by Henry Micheels on her wedding day. The Cohens were manufacturers, wholesalers and retailers of clocks in The Hague. A family tradition sustained.

- The telephone directory of Jerusalem and Southern Palestine from January 1946.

- Moshe Hananel, *The Jerusalemites: A Journey through the British Mandate Telephone Book, 1946*, published in Hebrew in Eretz Magazine (2007). The British Mandate's last telephone book was the source for Moshe Hananel's own book published in 2007. In it he wrote about many of the people, their families, successes, intrigues, scandals, love affairs, murders, thefts and related histories. It is a very rare heavily embossed leather-bound library and collector's item.

- Tirza published the history of her own family from her detailed research. Her grandparents had lived in Den Haag in the Netherlands. Their names were Margarethe Antje Cohen-Micheels born 29.3.1878 and Emanuel Micheels, born 2.3.1876 in Arnhem. Both were murdered on 13.5.1943 in Sobibor. The Nazis never gave details of the victims' graves. Tirza and her family have placed three small brass plaques embedded on the street outside her grand-parents last home at Prins Mauritslaan 75, Den Haag.

As we wandered through the house, we found ourselves browsing shelves filled with thousands of books and walls adorned with photographs of a younger Moshe. The images captured him alongside heads of state, business leaders, and notably with his close friend, the late King Hussein of Jordan, as well as the current King Abdullah and his wife.

On the third-floor rooftop terrace, we took in the views – a park on one side and a valley on the other. A life-size chessboard, with all its pieces in place, hinted at outdoor gatherings of family and friends over the years. The house itself was a reflection of their lives – modest yet rich in history. It was aged, full of their belongings and memories, with some parts cramped and creaking. The newer metal stair rails, leading to upper floors and a security shelter in the basement, added another layer to the story of this lived-in, storied home.

We settled into massive leather chairs, sipping tea and nibbling on nuts and fruit, while our hosts shared the stories of their lives – intimate, honest, filled with hope, yet deeply profound. Their family history, woven through wars, peace, and commerce, unfolded before us. This couple, with a deep understanding and empathy for others, has dedicated their lives to the principles of coexistence and peace. Apolitical, nonjudgmental, and altruistic, they've chosen to live and let live, making the world a better place. I'm proud to call them my friends.

That day, sitting in their home, I felt immense gratitude. Denis had supported me in taking the risk to visit, to witness firsthand the lives they've built. Without him, this experience would never have been possible. As a token of appreciation, they gifted Denis a rare black-and-white Italian etching, which he carefully carried back to Ireland. It now hangs proudly in his home in Wicklow.

Eventually, we were dropped off at our hotel, with so much on which to reflect. The evening offered a welcome pause, giving me time to process it all. Later, Yuval Hananel, the couple's second son, came by the hotel, and he and Denis headed out for the night.

Denis: a beer with Yuval

To have visited Tirza and Moshe's home was a privilege. They were such interesting and kind people and their home was full of fascinating art and books. They told us about their family histories in Bulgaria and The Netherlands (and the horrors they had faced), and how they came to be born in Israel. It is hard for me to put myself in their shoes given all that has happened to Jewish people down through the centuries.

Like all Israelis, Tirza and Moshe had been in the army. They have witnessed unspeakable violence and have put their lives at risk for their country and their compatriots. They built hugely successful tourism businesses together and employed hundreds of people and worked to foster cooperation across communities. The story of Israel and Israelis is inspiring when viewed from the perspective of people like them.

That evening they arranged for me to meet their son Yuval for a beer. Yuval is a 34-year-old lawyer with two children. We chatted about our lives. He told me he had had PTSD from his time in the army after seeing his friends dying around him after a rocket hit their barracks. He had gone to take a shower and his life had been saved. I asked him what Israel meant to him. He said that when he went to travel, he was treated weirdly in European cities because people either didn't like Israelis or else they thought Jews controlled the media and so he was brought to meet leading politicians in Spain. He said Israel was the only place where he and his friends could feel safe and live their lives without being treated weirdly or persecuted.

In his own words: 'When I planned my Eurotrip I thought about myself as a citizen of the world – someone travelling to various places and going to meet people and experience new cultures. It very quickly became obvious that I would be received first and foremost as a Jew/Israeli. The first girl I was chatting with stopped talking to me when I said I was Jewish. I was brought to the Catalan Parliament because people I met believed I was an influential Jew and in practically every other place my identity was the key issue of the conversation. The core issue for me is that me being Jewish/Israeli was constantly an issue. Here I don't have that. My ancestry plays no role in my everyday life. Although I might be safer in a European country than I am here, the problem is that my identity would constantly be an issue.'

He is a liberal guy, an atheist. He didn't like the government he said – like many Israelis. And yet, he like so many others felt that the Israeli Defence Forces, the IDF, has had to do what they've had to do to try and get the hostages back and to try and kill Hamas fighters.

I responded that from what I had seen and heard on the news there is no way the army has acted in a disciplined manner with so many innocent lives lost (as well as some documented instances of intentional murder of innocents). He said the IDF were doing their best in the most difficult territory and that they had been killing one militant for every one civilian which was better than any other war. For example, he said, the Americans in Iraq had killed four civilians for every militant. He said he could show me proof for this. I took him at his word, not wanting to have an argument. He had been very kind and friendly. But I did Google this as soon as I went home, and the IDF figures were hugely disputed by numerous credible international news organisations.

At the time of writing, approximately 25,000 women and children have been killed out of a total number of 45,000 (although it is impossible to know for certain the exact numbers). The Jerusalem Post reported on 4 November 2024 that the number of Hamas militants killed has been recently revised down to 15,000 (from 19,000) by the IDF. Yuval now acknowledges that the true figure of militants to civilians killed is close to 1:2 not 1:1. According to Reuters on 8 November 2024, The U.N. Human Rights Office said that nearly 70% of the fatalities it has verified were women and children, and condemned what it called a systematic violation of the fundamental principles of international humanitarian law.

War is hell. Statistics are propaganda. How can anyone have a balanced and even-handed opinion?

I really liked Yuval, and admired how he and his family did their best to stay positive. We had a great time, chatting and getting to know each other in a hip Speakeasy bar that had no name. With great cocktails. The normality was incongruous – life goes on for those who can keep on living. It's not their fault, it's their good fortune. And mine. Others are less fortunate.

As we walked out from the pub to head for home, we stopped for a moment in front of a billboard with the faces of all the hostages which read #BringThemHomeNow. We paused to look at them and expressed the hope that they would be released, but knowing some wouldn't be so fortunate. It really hit home to me how much grief this situation must cause Israelis. We hugged and said our goodbyes

---

Day 4: Palestine (The West Bank)

We woke up the next morning to another beautiful, sunny day in Jerusalem. Ibrahim, our Palestinian guide, arrived at the decided time. He was a fit man and was born in 1968. We chatted for a while and he told us that he offered private tours of the city and surrounding areas, including Acre, Haifa, Bethlehem and the West Bank. He was born in a centuries old house, in the Old City of Jerusalem.

Ibrahim our Palestinian Guide:

Good morning from Jerusalem

Some information about me.

Born in the old city of Jerusalem 1968 in a few hundred-years-old house. I experienced the meaning of the place from the beginning. The different people, the different cultures and religions in that tiny place and noticing that everyone is ignoring the other and ignorant about the others, only seeing them walking by without saying Hi even.

After high school, I decided to study languages and history which I did in a Palestinian university. At the age of 25, I decided to study Hebrew and only after that I was able to communicate with jews for the first time. Only then did I realise the importance of understanding the same language which should never be only translated words but what is behind that language: religion, history, culture and politics and that was what motivated me to study history, political science, tour guiding and international relations, specialised in Christianity,

Realising the common human threads between different people are way more than the differences, I started having interfaith groups and mixed groups trying to expose them to to experience the things we have in common sometimes for the first time,

I have one boy and three girls. My son Faisal is a third-year medicine student in Jerusalem, my daughter Natal is a second-year medicine student too, my Nuran just finished high school and is planning to study medicine and the fourth, Nurcin, is in 8th grade.

Living in Jerusalem. offers the kind of experience which is different from any other place in the whole world. It is the place where you can feel connected, where all your senses and your mind work so hard trying to put things together and collect everything you know about your history, your faith and your politics and the relationship between. All these great events that shaped our lives, our history and our future and the greatest figures: Abraham, David, Solomon, Jesus, Mohammad, all of them in one place.

The events that start from the beginning with the foundation, and will be ended when the Messiah, will be entering the Golden Gate, to the stage of the resurrection and judgement; Jewish, Christian and Moslem cemeteries, theatre of dead people that wait patiently, thinking of all the dead, a life that wait that still shape our life, our actions and our policies all around the world.

Thinking of what should be getting people together, is that same thing that keeps them apart, thinking of the power of ignorance and how to use it to achieve different purposes.

In that small, tiny city you can experience the smells, the sounds, the calls for prayers, the bells and the holy places.

This is only part of it.

The city that you can easily fall in love with, not easy love but it's the ultimate love that you cannot explain, it will always have a special place in your mind and heart.

You will always be connected to the other word mainly because this place is the closest place to heaven and the only gate. That power and energy all in one spot and everything we know was shaped by that source of energy of the presence of God.

This particular morning Denis is going to take a tour on his own to the West Bank including Bethlehem with Ibrahim. The West Bank, named for its location west of the River Jordan, is the largest section of the now broken up Palestine. It is territorially separate from the much smaller Gaza strip. The mainstay of its economy is agriculture.

Denis's Thoughts On His Visit To Palestine

The West Bank

Moshe has the most twinkling eyes. Eyes that charm and disarm and reset the person looking back at him. He and Tirza had planned our trip with such care – they wanted to show us their country from as many perspectives as possible. They organised for us to take a tour with their Palestinian friend, Ibrahim. He spoke with such intelligence and passion about Jerusalem and what it means to all traditions as we drove through the morning traffic. We then drove towards an ugly, fortified wall separating East and West Jerusalem (the 'Separation Barrier' stretches for 700km through the West Bank restricting the movement of over 3 million Palestinians; Israel says the wall is for security purposes). Ibrahim stopped the car, and we stood outside, and he pointed at the houses high on the hill and said: 'They are the illegal Israeli settlements.'

He showed me a map of the West Bank with all of the settlements scattered throughout. He continued: 'That's the difficulty with a two state solution – there is no easy way to divide the land to make a workable Palestinian state. The settlements have been the policy of Israeli governments for many years'. In 2016 a

UN Security Council resolution stated that the settlements constituted a flagrant violation of International Law.

There are now 146 illegal settlements with approximately 700,000 settlers in the West Bank. There are 3.3 million Palestinians living there. Some of the Jewish settlers came from Russia and other Eastern European countries (where they had faced worsening persecution) and built houses in the West Bank because it was much cheaper than elsewhere. Other Israelis moved to the West Bank for religious reasons - Ultraorthodox Jews form one-third of all settlers. Many are armed. Israel now illegally occupies 60% of the West Bank, with 18% under Palestinian control and 22% under joint Israeli-Palestinian control (source UN OCHA).

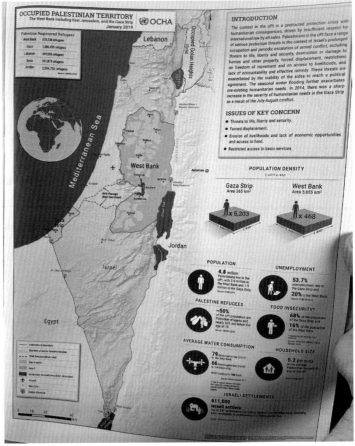

Map showing Israeli settlements & occupied land in blue; territory under Palestinian control
in orange

We drove up to the checkpoint festooned with barbed wire and heavily guarded by soldiers and guns. We were allowed through after passport checks. There were no other cars going in either direction. It was eerie.

Mural of Shireen Abu Akleh

As we drove into Palestinian territory, we stopped to look at a famous stretch of the wall. It was painted with a number of large murals including an image of actor Morgan Freeman (who played Nelson Mandela) alongside a quote by the former South African president: 'We know too well that our freedom is incomplete without the freedom of the Palestinians', and movingly – a mural of Shireen Abu Akleh – the Arab-American journalist that was killed in 2022. Abu Akleh (1971 – 2022) was a prominent Palestinian-American journalist who worked as a reporter for 25 years for Al Jazeera, before she was killed by Israeli forces while wearing a blue press vest and covering a raid on the Jenin refugee camp in the Israeli-occupied West Bank. Abu Akleh was one of the most prominent names across the Middle East for her decades of reporting in the Palestinian territories and seen as a role model for many Arab and Palestinian women. She is considered to be an icon of Palestinian journalism.

At the time of writing, since the start of the Gaza war, according to the Committee to Protect Journalists: 160 journalists have been killed including 129 Palestinians, two Israelis and six Lebanese, with scores more injured and arrested.

Banksy artwork on the wall in the West Bank

Beside the wall there was a Banksy art installation called the *Walled Off Hotel*; it was closed now as there were almost no tourists. Ibrahim then showed me a Banksy artwork of two angels with crowbars attempting to prise open the wall and another of a dove in the crosshairs of a shooter.

We drove into Bethlehem. Honestly, I didn't know what to expect. It was a well-developed town built from a bright cream stone. There were some people in the square as we drove towards the Church of the Nativity and there were Palestinian police officers and Palestinian soldiers, who have control of some, but not all, of the West Bank. Ibrahim and I chatted with the Police Officers, and they were full of smiles and welcomes. It gave me great hope to see Palestinian people in control of Palestinian territory and imagine a future where two States co-exist together peacefully.

Meeting Palestinian Police Officers in Bethlehem

We parked and walked up to the Church. There were no queues. There were no tourists. Again, it was hard to imagine how people continued to keep going, to feed their families when their sources of income had disappeared. We walked in silence through the Church and down into the Grotto. The stone before the place of His birth was rubbed worn by centuries of bent knees. I knelt, I felt and prayed. I'm a believer, not in any one denomination but in the monotheistic ideals of faith and love and understanding and tolerance and peace from which the Christian, Muslim and Jewish communities were born. The sacred wonder of this place cannot be overstated.

The entrance to the birthplace of Jesus

At the birthplace of Jesus

We went into the gift shop. It was their first day opening for four months. I bought a crib for my housemate and friend Annie who LOVES Christmas. The shopkeepers asked me where I was from. 'Ireland,' I replied, prompting lots of hugs and handshakes. The Palestinian people are hugely appreciative of the love and support they have received from Ireland. Ibrahim and I then went for some food in a small restaurant on the main Square as normal life went on around us – chats, laughter, cool cars, handshakes and hugs. We ate falafel, shakshuka (poached eggs and tomatoes), hummus and musakhan (chicken and spices). The flavours were sumptuous.

When we met up again later that evening, I asked Moshe whether he believed Jesus was born in Bethlehem and he said: 'If it happened right there or a few hundred yards away or even somewhere else entirely, it doesn't matter. There are over a thousand years of tears wept there.'

After Denis went off, I decided to avail of the free day to get a decent walk. There would be no tour for me today, just time to wander and explore at my own pace. There was certainly plenty to muse about.

As I left our hotel, I could see the lobby was a hive of activity. The additional security was notable with walkie-talkies everywhere. Outside in the grounds, barriers had been erected and the gate was screened off from outside observers. There were TV crews and blacked out VIP vans. This was Easter Saturday in the Eastern and Orthodox Christian calendar – a big religious feast day.

This is a very important event which occurs every year at the Church of the Holy Sepulchre in Jerusalem on this Saturday and believers travel from around the globe to attend.

At the King David Hotel

I had a most enjoyable time that morning taking in the bustle of the city as it was preparing for the influx of pilgrims. I decided to walk to the King David Hotel for a coffee. Here also the security was palpable. They did let me in, even with my walking pole. It appeared they had a high-level group from Russia as guests.

I wandered out to the terrace, overlooking the city, the pool and gardens. It was surprisingly empty at this hour. I asked for a double espresso but was offered Turkish filtered or instant coffee. I ordered a filter. The guest services manager wandered by and stopped to chat. It appears that before Covid and retirement, he was the regional manager for Royal Jordanian Airlines. He said that the hotel occupancy had plummeted since October and the hotel had to close for several months over the New Year. Something unheard of in its history. It was now running at around 15% occupancy. He asked me who I was visiting. When I mentioned our hosts he told me he knew them well. When I tried to pay for my coffee, there was no charge. We parted with the head of security taking our picture at the front of the hotel.

As I walked back to our hotel at Notre Dame Centre, the streets were now packed. The city of Jerusalem, like most cities in the event of major gatherings of people, was in full swing – preparation stage, steel barriers on the sidewalks, light rail suspended, traffic diverted, soldiers with guns and a large police presence. The crowds were multiplying. Leaning, pushing forward on their toes, craning for a view, children on fathers' shoulders. There were TV crews from all over the world – Russian, American, European, Israeli, Al Jazeera, Ethiopian and so many more, all running live commentary and interviews. This was all being played out against the backdrop of the Old City walls and the entrance to the Old City via the New Gate. It was building up to the crescendo of celebrations in the Church of the Holy Sepulchre. The big screens dotted all around, provided coverage of what was happening inside but with the bright sunlight, it was hard to see.

I arrived back in the hotel and Denis and Ibrahim also returned, full of their own day's experiences. Ibrahim then said we would have to go to try to get in and see the events in the Church of The Holy Sepulchre.

We later read that, 'The Holy Fire' is an ancient Orthodox Christian ceremony held annually on Holy Saturday at the Church of the Holy Sepulchre in Jerusalem which is believed to be the site of Jesus' crucifixion and resurrection. During the ritual, the Greek Orthodox Patriarch emerges from the tomb with a lit candle, symbolising a miraculous flame, which is then shared among the congregation. This event, steeped in tradition for over a millennium, often attracts thousands, despite recent restrictions due to safety concerns amid ongoing regional tensions. The Holy Sepulchre is shared by six denominations: Greek Orthodox, Latin Catholics, Armenian Orthodox, Copts, Ethiopian, and Syrian-Jacobites. Interestingly, the inner part of the church is shared by Catholics or Christians in general. The key to the church is held by Muslims.

On that day the only way to enter the Old City was with a special pass. The main ceremonies were ending when we arrived, but our trusted guide found a way through. Ibrahim hurriedly led us past the stalls, the souk-like shops and within minutes we were at the entrance courtyard of the Holy Sepulchre. As people were coming out, we managed to slide inside.

Inside was a frenzy of activity. Children and adults all dressed up and carried bunches of long thin flaming candles, tapers and blazing torches. It felt like a swirling inferno of humanity straight out of the mediaeval era.

The Tomb of Jesus: Site of His burial and resurrection (Church of the Holy Sepulchre)

The Anointing Stone where Jesus was prepared for burial (Church of the Holy Sepulchre)

We got within metres of all the action, standing behind the TV cameras area. In my entire life I have never witnessed anything like it. The blazing torches everywhere with masses of people heaving and swaying made it scary but breathtaking. We felt that we had attended some sacred, historic ritual. For many of the people present, this was the culmination of their lifetime spiritual aspirations as Christians. We thought it must be like a Christian Hajj. Sometimes it felt like a meeting of different Christian strands. The chants, singing, and prayers rang out as each sect from all corners of the globe had their own procession, all in a very confined space circling the inner church sanctum. Myriads of colours assailed my eyes with golds, reds, black, yellows, richly embroidered and gold tassel banners and strange clerical headgear. As they reached the entrance each group stopped, waited to respect the protocol of only three people at a time, entering the Holy of Holies. We moved around the back and bought a bunch of thin candles. We lit them from a sacred torch and then queued to kneel, present our candles and kiss the consecrated stone at the rear of the small sanctum.

The area was closely guarded by the various religious groupings who share present day control of this church.

We eventually left and back up the narrow-cobbled stone streets through the thinning crowds, to our hotel. That night we dined overlooking the city. We booked flights home for May 7th from Tel Aviv. Both of us were overwhelmed with the pace so far but nothing could have prepared us for the next day. Catching up with the news that evening in the papers, news wires were filled with hopeful bulletins about a Gaza ceasefire.

Denis's thoughts:

I had seen the Holy Fire Ceremony before on TV, but never thought I would be there in real life. It is like the Superbowl for Christians (with tickets for the event changing hands for up to €10,000). A priest we met told us he had tried to attend for over 20 years and it was a dream come true for him to be there. To see the passion of people as they passed the flame to one another around the Church of the Holy

Sepulchre and through the streets of the Old City was amazing! It is then flown to churches in Athens, Belgrade, Kyiv, Cairo, Moscow, Bucharest and elsewhere! It is said that the fire emerges miraculously and is lit by the Holy Spirit. Beside the tomb of Jesus we watched a procession of clergy from the Armenian, Coptic, Syrian, Greek and Russian Christian churches. Each with their own costumes and hats and chants and incense. It was unlike anything I've seen anywhere. A true once-in-a-lifetime experience. Both Dad and I knew as it was happening just how special it was. We would never have made it so close if there had been the normal numbers of tourists. And it was all thanks to Ibrahim who expertly guided us through the crowds right up to what was a front-row vantage point. We were thrilled, buzzing.

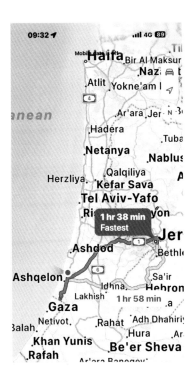

Day 5: May 5th

Ashkelon – Barzilai Medical Centre – The Yad Vashem Holocaust Memorial

Early next morning on Sunday May 5th, Tirza and Moshe were at the door to take us to the port city of Ashkelon/Ashqelon, about 77 km south-west of Jerusalem. Ashkelon is on the Mediterranean coast and nearly 20 km from the border with Gaza. Our destination was not Ashkelon itself but the hospital nearby called the Barzilai Medical Centre. There we would meet an amazing Jewish couple, Dr Ron Lobel and his wife, Judith Lobel, who have lived their lives quite literally on the edge, on the border between Israel and Gaza, tending to the sick and injured, irrespective of where they come from.

This day will forever be etched in our memory.

Ron & Yudithe

As we drove into Ashkelon, we found a thriving, expanding city. There were lots of new high-rise apartments overlooking the Mediterranean coastline. The current population is over 150,000. In 1961, the population was a mere 24,000.

The city is the northern terminus for the Trans-Israel oil pipeline from Eilat on the Red Sea to the Mediterranean port. Interestingly, it is also the site of the largest seawater reverse osmosis (SWRO desalination plant) – the largest plant of its kind in the world. Additionally, Ashkelon is the home to the brewery that supplies Carlsberg and Tuborg to the Israeli market.

Barzilai Medical Centre and Dr Ron

We kept driving until we reached the Barzilai Medical Centre. Established in 1961, it is a 600 bed, general hospital that provides a wide range of medical services to a population of 580,000. Given its proximity to Gaza Strip just six miles away, it is particularly noted for its emergency care with protocols in place for wartime operations. The hospital has been the target of numerous rockets, fired from inside Gaza, sometimes as many as 140 in one weekend. To say this medical centre plays a vital role in treating emergency cases is an understatement.

The hospital has a staff of 3,000 of whom 65% are Palestinian. We were met outside by Dr Ron, whose hospital title is Director of Emergency and Disaster Management. He showed us around, chatting straightforwardly. He told us that he had worked for decades in public emergency medicine before the public administration of Gaza was handed over in May 1994 to Palestinians supervision as part of the Oslo Accords. I was interested to hear that he was the 1994 Weizmann Scholar graduate from Harvard Kennedy School of Government – my own alma mater. Dr Lobel had also contributed to setting up hospitals in Gaza and also runs joint projects between Palestinian and Israeli doctors.

The Prayer Space

Hussein ibn Ali's 11th Century Mosque

As part of our visit, Dr Ron brought us to an open-air Muslim mosque/praying area built on a raised mound at the back of the hospital compound. The small simple structure was an area of 50m x 50m, enclosed by beautifully carved marble walls, about 1m in height. The marble had been sourced in various locations including Italy, India, China and Macedonia. It was built in the early 2000s, not only as a place of worship for Muslim patients and staff but also for pilgrims from all over the world. As we stood around, Dr Ron commented: 'This is an island of Shi'ite Muslim prayer in an Israeli hospital in a Jewish state. It really is unique.' He explained that the mosque's establishment is part of the hospital's commitment to serving a multi-ethnic, multi-religious population and that Muslim links with this particular site go back a long way.

We were intrigued and wanted to know more. The story that unfolded was, to us, quite astonishing. It all began with the grandson of Prophet Mohammed called Hussein ibn Ali (628-680 CE) and where his head was buried. The Barzilai Medical Centre is connected to the site of the Hussein ibn Ali 11th Century Mosque, a centre for Muslim pilgrimages which was destroyed by the Israeli army in 1950. Dr Ron told the story that in the early 2000s, a Shi'ite spiritual leader arrived at the hospital asking for permission to build a prayer area for pilgrims. From his research, he believed he knew the exact location of where the original Mosque had stood (Hussein ibn Ali's head had been interred there for some time before being moved). Digging began at the mound at the back of the hospital and after going down about a metre or so, they came upon a cornerstone which turned out to be that of the ancient mosque destroyed by the Crusaders. Shi'ites from around the globe funded the construction, particularly the Menasche David family who originated in Bagdad.

Then we discovered that this sacred site on which we stood had led to conflict and war in places like Syria and Iraq. A Reuters' report of 2015 explained:

> '...The Barzilai Medical Centre in the coastal town of Ashkelon is home to a tomb where, in the view of some Shi'ite Muslims, the head of Hussein ibn Ali, grandson of the Prophet Mohammed, lay interred for centuries following his death in battle... the worshippers' leader, Sheikh Moiz Tarmal, told Reuters. 'And we believe that if we pray here, God will listen to you.' The slaying of Hussein in the seventh century Battle of Karbala fuelled the split between Sunni and Shi'ite Muslims that has recently erupted with renewed ferocity in conflicts in Iraq and Syria... Particularly involving a religious group called Dawoodi Bohra, a Shi'ite sect with around a million adherents worldwide. Its members come annually on pilgrimage to the ornate marble enclosure marking the tomb on a grassy hillock within the Barzilai campus...Moshe Hananel, an Israeli scholar who helps arrange the Barzilai visits, said some of the Shi'ite pilgrims who flock to the hospital come from countries that do not recognise Israel. 'Their entry is approved in advance,' he said, declining to name specific countries due to the political sensitivities.'

What is it about religions, founded on the belief that people should love one another, yet end up in eternal conflict and mutual destruction?

October 7th and the Aftermath

At this point Dr Ron invited us to meet his wife, Judith. We travelled together to his home which was about 6km away. As we drove out from the hospital, the view to the right was of the coast and full of sand dunes with no houses or buildings nearby. The nearest signs of habitation were a few kilometres away in Gaza. In the distance, we could see fields that were clearly being farmed and cultivated. In general, however, the immediate area at the northern end of Gaza, where it borders Israel, is a wasteland. It is also the location of Gaza's northern crossing point with Israel, called the Erez Crossing.

The Lobel home is situated in a small, securely gated enclave right on the Gaza border. Judith showed us the wall at the end of their back garden – the 30 metre high Peace Wall built to protect the community from rockets from Gaza. Just 150m from this wall was another imposing wall – the border with Gaza which separates the Israelis and Palestinians. When the Israeli army was building the Peace Wall, Judith was asked the colours she would like it painted. She wanted flowers and so she got flowers. Other parts of this wall that stretch as far as the eye can see have murals and adornments of mosaics and children's art work. A most human endeavour to create beauty even in direst of circumstances.

The Peace Wall

View of the Peace Wall and Gaza from Ron & Yudithe's upstairs window

The Peace Wall built to protect from rocket attacks

The October 7th attack was foremost on everyone's mind.

The day we drove to the Lobel home, we commented that the area towards Gaza seemed to us to be like a no-man's-land. But it was from this no-man's-land, that a major part of the October 7th intrusion came. When we arrived, they had workmen in the house. Seven months after the October 7th Hamas invasion, the damage caused to their home was still being repaired. New windows were now reinforced with bullet-proof 90mm glass and a new steel frame inserted to protect the roof. As we chatted, Ron and Judith calmly told their story of that life-defining day. Ron had been interviewed many times by the international media, including Fox News and CNN. He talked about the jolt of shock, as they realised their home was under attack. He explained how they fled to the secure bomb-proof basement where they were ensconced for ten hours with no electricity and no water. Each minute, he said, seemed like a lifetime as they waited for the Israeli army to come to their aid. His immediate concern was for the hospital, and he stayed in contact with his colleagues throughout the attack. Even as he chatted, we heard rockets and gunfire in the distance. The hospital itself was not attacked but in Ron's words he, 'experienced the most dramatic day of its life.' Because of his role as director of emergencies, was kept up to speed at all times. Protocols were immediately put into action, for example, getting patients to underground secure areas and this had to be done as the dead and injured arrived. Many of the staff lived in surrounding villages and couldn't get in to help. That day, over 400 casualties were treated at the hospital. He said about 90 arrived dead and with only 10 operating theatres, some were stabilised and sent on to other hospitals in Israel. As soon as he could escape from their home, Ron and his team were back in the hospital treating the victims – Israelis and Palestinians alike.

They talked about the trauma in their own community which he described as a big issue. He talked of the people from neighbouring villages, dead, injured or taken as hostages. They both described how their Buddhism was central to their daily living on an international war border. But they were both adamant that this is where they would stay. They raised their family here and said: 'It is their forever home.'

As Ron said, describing their beliefs, 'We studied Buddhism for many years, and we always say that we have our feet in Judaism and our wings in Buddhism. One of the basic teachings of Buddhism is that everything is flexible, everything is changing everything, and you never know what is to come. But you have the illusion of knowing your future and you need a certain certainty in order to continue living. The 7th of October and what came afterwards made it really clear that we have no clue about the future.'

Ron continued about the people of Gaza, his neighbours: 'I worked for six years in Gaza and I know that the people I've met in Gaza are peaceful people. All they want is to get up in the morning and send the children to school and then go to the gates of the school to get them back in one piece at 4pm in the afternoon. I am lucky to have enough money to put bread on the table. But they are all under the rule of Hamas which is the rule of Iran.'

Denis's thoughts:

The Shrine at the hospital

I don't think I've ever enjoyed the conversation of anyone as much as I enjoyed Moshe's. He was warm, wise, contrary, funny, profound, trivial, informative, playful. In quick succession or even simultaneously. It warmed my heart to see the genuine affection and respect between him and Dad. He had been hugely successful in his tourism career – responsible for bringing over 300,000 visitors to Israel each year. He had also had business and health challenges in recent years which must have shaken him, but he showed zero hint of self-pity. Of all his many achievements, one he seemed most proud of was the role he played in having the shrine built at the hospital in Ashkelon. He and Tirza (and Ron who ran the hospital and who had previously run many hospitals in Gaza before the Israelis withdrew in 2006) had to really fight to have various stakeholders agree to the building of a shrine at this holy place for Shi'ite Muslims in the grounds of an Israeli hospital. Dad and I knelt and said a brief prayer in the beautifully designed and simple outdoor Muslim prayer space made from gleaming white marble, gorgeously decorated. To see Moshe, Tirza, Ron and Dad sitting on the marble bench overlooked by a magnificent tree, looking at this space for prayer and contemplation built by Jewish people in collaboration with Muslim people, I was moved and felt hopeful and optimistic.

The wall near the Northern Gates of Gaza

Later that day, a few kilometres from the hospital, we were standing just 300m from the wall of Gaza just 50 metres from Dr. Ron's house. Tears had streamed down my cheeks and Dad's hearing about the murder of 20 of Ron and Yudithe's neighbours on 7 October and how they had had to hide petrified from the attackers under their house. I cried again looking towards Gaza thinking about the thousands upon thousands of innocent dead and injured women, men and children and their loved ones who are unable to even grieve properly because they are trying to avoid being killed themselves by guns, bombs or starvation. There was a Path to Peace wall beside their house (a wall built to give extra protection from rockets and gunfire), which was decorated by Israeli children with hearts and doves and lots of youthful hope and love and beautiful naivety. It seemed to me standing there that the Israeli political and military leaders were recklessly affecting these children's future, by turning the world against their people and by creating a new generation of Palestinian orphans who could possibly turn to violence in the future.

Perhaps I didn't know enough, and maybe I don't know enough to comment now. I had listened to Israelis say, 'it's cool and hip to hate Jews now' and 'these protesting American kids are just watching TikTok and haven't got a clue what's going on here', but I don't agree that it's as simple as that – I think it is understandable for people around the world to express anger and revulsion at what they see as indiscriminate killings of defenceless people by those with unimaginable power.

Anger is something Ron and Yudithe have had to deal with daily since the atrocities of 7 October. They are Buddhists (from Jewish heritage) and Ron had managed hospitals in Israel and in the Gaza Strip. He had trained many Arab doctors and had seen his efforts to strengthen cross-community cooperation fall apart when Israel ceded control of Gaza in 2005 which was then taken over by Hamas. He said to us, "We consider the Palestinians across the border not as enemies. We consider them as neighbours.".

We sat and drank tea and ate fruit in the home that they were trying to make a home again. I asked Ron if he could understand how many in the West felt Israel had lost its soul in how it was conducting itself in war, especially using starvation as a weapon of war. Did he acknowledge that was the case? He said he did, and he did understand, and he said he disagreed with many of the actions of the military. But he did ask me to consider this: 'If your children were in a school targeted by rockets from a school on their side, would you fire rockets back at the school to prevent your children being killed if it meant killing their children?'

He held my hands as I wept, and I said I couldn't possibly answer his question as it's hypothetical so any answer I gave would be pointless and self-serving – I couldn't say with honesty how I would feel in their shoes.

As Ron was talking we heard gunfire ring out, and rockets launched... at first I felt uneasy, knowing someone maybe dying, someone maybe killing... but then it became background noise. I guess people can ignore what they must to keep going.

Yudithe points towards Gaza.

Ron and Yudithe told us how they tried to feel compassion for those who saw them as enemies and not let themselves fall prey to anger. How every day they tried to let go of anger and negativity, and how it was very hard sometimes, but that through their Buddhist practices they attempted to do so. It was so noble. Yudith showed us her bookcase with books about Childhood trauma. She worked with young children to help them cope with the horrors which had happened around them. Herself and Ron had suffered such sadness and tragedy, and yet they remained so resilient and kind too. These were special people.

No doubt, the stories we heard will resonate with those who have lived in so many war-torn parts of the world. This knowledge though, cannot diminish in any way, the horrors faced by those we met that day. If it did, then where is our humanity?

We said our goodbyes and went back 6 km to Ashkelon. We parked near the seafront and had lunch at the water's edge, against the backdrop of the marina with sailboats and yachts. It was hard to make the mental and psychological transition. As we watched a group of excited children, with their life jackets on, were about to start their sailing lessons, while teenagers on skateboards straddled the boardwalk – all so full of life and excitement. We heard a rocket in the far distance but those on the beach or in the surrounding restaurants and coffee shops didn't even blink an eye.

This was a parallel universe.

Holocaust Remembrance at Yad Vashem

Back we went to Jerusalem, and we had just enough time to get changed for the Opening Ceremony of Holocaust Martyrs' and Heroes' Remembrance Day at Yad Vashem. The Yad Vashem Museum is on a 18-hectare complex and is Israel's official memorial to the victims of the Holocaust. Accompanied by our hosts, we passed through all the police and army checkpoints into the VIP parking area. From there we were brought through and into the large, floodlit, outdoor space with about 1,000 people already in place. The back half of the area was occupied by young members of the armed and security forces. They all looked so youthful, 18–30-year-olds. Around the perimeter, discreet security was everywhere. In front of us was the area reserved for special international and diplomatic invitees. There were several large screens, and we were provided with earpieces to hear the translations of the speakers and the masters of ceremonies.

Netanyahu speaks

Holocaust survivors with their families

It started at precisely 8pm. The introduction to the evening was followed by a number of speeches and interspersed with filmed testimonies of individual survivors who were on the stage – probably the last living survivors of the Holocaust.

Listening to the stories reminded me of the extent to which the current Israeli population derives from the international resettlement of refugees, immigrants and international protection applicants from all over Europe, North Africa and elsewhere. Natives from so many different cultures, nationalities and ethnicities – displaced, persecuted and unified by a common belief in Judaism. It seemed to me that the Israelis are unified by a common religion but in contrast, their Palestinian Arab neighbours are primarily united by bloodlines, tribes and the claim to have lived on these lands for a millennia. As we know, particularly from Northern Ireland, this is a very potent and inflammable mix.

The platform speakers included the president of Israel Isaac Herzog, son of a previous president, the Irish-born Chaim Herzog, the Prime Minister Benjamin Netanyahu, the Chief Justice, the Chief Rabbi and others. This is the event that Mr Netanyahu used to issue a strong message to the world. This is how Associated Press reported on this night that we witnessed:

> *Israeli Prime Minister Benjamin Netanyahu on Sunday rejected international pressure to halt the war in Gaza in a fiery speech marking the country's annual Holocaust Memorial Day, declaring: 'If Israel is forced to stand alone, Israel will stand alone.'*
>
> *The message, delivered in a setting that typically avoids politics, was aimed at the growing chorus of world leaders who have criticised the heavy toll caused by Israel's military offensive against Hamas militants and have urged the sides to agree to a cease-fire.*
>
> *Netanyahu has said he is open to a deal that would pause nearly seven months of fighting and bring home hostages held by Hamas. But he also says he remains committed to an invasion of the southern Gaza city of Rafah, despite widespread international opposition because of the more than 1 million civilians huddled there.*

'I say to the leaders of the world: No amount of pressure, no decision by any international forum will stop Israel from defending itself,' he said, speaking in English. 'Never again is now.'

Yom HaShoah, the day Israel observes as a memorial for the 6 million Jews killed by Nazi Germany and its allies in the Holocaust, is one of the most solemn dates on the country's calendar. Speeches at the ceremony generally avoid politics, though Netanyahu in recent years has used the occasion to lash out at Israel's archenemy Iran.

We discovered that the remembrance began that morning with the sounding of a siren for two minutes throughout the entire country. For the duration of the hearing, work was halted, people stopped walking in the streets, cars pulled off to the side of the road and everybody stood silently in reverence to the victims of the Holocaust. Afterwards, the focus of the ceremony at Yad Vashem was the laying of wreaths at the foot of the six torches by dignitaries and the representatives of survivor groups and institutions. The evening lasted over two hours.

It was freezing cold that night at Yad Vashem.

Perhaps an omen.

Denis's thoughts:

Visiting Yad Vashem

That evening we found ourselves at Yad Vashem. The level of security was impressive – helicopters, snipers, metal detectors, armed soldiers etc. Walking slowly through security I got chatting with a lady in a wheelchair and her daughter. The older lady – Giselle Cycowicz – had been in Auschwitz and had met Joe Biden at Yad Vashem in 2022. She had the sweetest smile and accepted my offer of my jumper to keep her hands warm as she said she was cold.

Her daughter asked me where we were from. I said Ireland. She said she was surprised we were there, because the Irish are no longer friends of Israel. I replied that Ireland tries to support justice for all and we were honoured to be there at the Holocaust Remembrance event.

With Holocaust survivor Giselle Cycowicz

The event itself was a very solemn affair with dignified speeches from the Chief Rabbi and the President of Israel followed by what seemed to me to be a recklessly intransigent political speech by Prime Minister Netanyahu that was inappropriate for the occasion. Listening to him use the event for his own ends was disturbing. No one applauded any of the speeches (as is customary at the event) which made it difficult to gauge the feelings of the many hundreds in the crowd.

After that though, the event was moving beyond words as a number of Holocaust survivors told their harrowing and inspiring stories via video on large screens and then walked or were helped to light torches on the stage. It was quite something to see the lives they have lived since they survived the Concentration Camps and to see them now surrounded by their extended families at their advanced ages. They have survived and thrived in the State of Israel. It was heart-warming to hear their tales and sitting beside Moshe and Tirza (both of whom lost family in the Holocaust), I could completely understand their love for Israel and the lives they have been able to live because of its existence. But I did not know how to feel about it all, and reflecting months later I still don't.

One people's battle (and sins) to survive led to another people's misery and effective incarceration. Is it possible to feel hopeful and devastated at the same time about the two very different sides of the same coin?

It seems to me that the whole situation is an affront to justice and humanity. But there are also many good people on all sides also, who co-exist peacefully, or who work for peace, but they don't get the same level of attention (it would make me happy if more people knew about Martin and his friends – Jewish Israelis putting themselves at risk to prevent Palestinian farmers being attacked by settlers and having their land taken). Every conversation reveals a perspective which can be hard to fathom from an Irish standpoint, but we can never know how we would feel in someone else's shoes. I kept seeking hope and optimism and kept hearing complications and justifications and entrenched divisions. Ultimately, language and religion and war can seem like insurmountable barriers to compromise. But humans have always found ways to adapt and co-exist after conflict – maybe we can live in hope that new leaders will emerge who can stop the bloodshed and find common ground and compromise. Soon please God.

On Monday May 6th, we left Jerusalem. Before we checked out of the hotel, we were shown up to the third floor to view the current project in the centre's development. It will be open to the public in 2025. The large windowless rectangular room circa 30m X 40m with a high ceiling is to be the Pentecost Hall.

According to the pamphlet:

> 'The Pentecost Hall is an immersive 360° work of art that represents the Jewish Feast of Shavuot and the first Christian Pentecost at the Cenacle at Mt. Zion. Such a gathering for Shavuot would be the norm as Jewish people travelled to Jerusalem for centuries to give thanks for the harvest of the first fruit.
>
> Pentecost is one of the Great feasts in the Eastern Orthodox Church, a Solemnity in the Roman Rite of the Catholic Church, a Festival in the Lutheran Churches, and a Principal Feast in the Anglican Communion.'

Segment of Pentecost artwork

Basilica of the Annunciation, Nazareth (exterior)

Inside the Basilica of the Annuciation

Regina Palestine

Day 6

Nazareth – Capernaum – Sea of Galilee – Tiberias

As we departed Jerusalem, we reminisced on the lifetime of experiences we packed into a few short days. It felt like we had been in the city for extraordinarily special dates particularly Orthodox Easter and the Holocaust memorial. All against the backdrop of a country at war.

With Tirza, again at the wheel, we whizzed by a maze of new motorways and tunnels under construction. There is a massive midtown development underway in Jerusalem as you travel north on the main highway. On our right as we drove was the West Bank. We drove for nearly two hours until we reached our first destination – Nazareth.

Known as the Arab capital of Israel, Nazareth has a population of approximately 78,000, of whom 69% are Muslim andd 31% Christian. When we visited, the streets were narrow, and parking was chaotic. Many of the shops looked dilapidated, with many abandoned. Since the war in Gaza, religious tourism has vanished and there is no other leisure industry there. The area outside the local tourist office across from the church was sadly littered with rubbish.

The Encyclopaedia Britannica describes the city thus:

> *'Nazareth, historic city of Lower Galilee, in northern Israel; it is the largest Arab city of the country. In the New Testament Nazareth is associated with Jesus as his boyhood home and in its synagogue he preached the sermon that led to his rejection by his fellow townsmen. The city is now a centre of Christian pilgrimage. Christian Arabs now form about a third of the population.*
>
> *Modern Nazareth is a regional market and trade centre for the Arabs of Galilee; tourism and light manufacturing are also important. Many workers commute to industrial jobs in the Haifa Bay area and to agricultural and construction work in the Jewish settlements of the Plain of Esdraelon.'*

For visitors to Nazareth, it is mostly about its churches. According to the Bible it was the village where Jesus grew up and where he lived with Mary and Joseph. It is very much associated with The Annunciation, when Archangel Gabriel appeared to Mary to tell her that she would become the mother of Jesus. The two main churches here are linked to these biblical stories.

Our first stop was the Basilica of The Annunciation. Its area was so quiet that we drove right up to the door of the Basilica. At the entrance the notice from the Israel Ministry of Tourism – Israel Government Tourist Corporation – Nazareth Municipality says: *Historians say that the Grotto and its surroundings, being the site of the Annunciation, were turned into a worship place in the 1st and 2nd Century. Early sources referred to the place as being, 'The House of the Virgin Mary.'*

The current basilica was built over the course of a decade during the 1950s/1960s. The older church had been destroyed in 1263 by Mamluk Sultan in his bid to drive out the remaining Crusaders from Palestine. In preparation for the reconstruction, Pope John XXIII decided to have an archaeological exploration carried out as it had never been done prior to this. What was revealed was a grotto surrounded by a 4th century church with a foundation stone from a previous century with the words *Hail Mary.* This is believed to be Mary's home where the angel visited her and has been preserved in the new basilica.

Nearby was the Church of Joseph which is built over the original ruins of Joseph's home and carpentry shop, and consequently over the home that Jesus knew growing up. Further underground are caves that were carved into limestone that were probably used for grain storage and water cisterns. We were the only people in the entire compound except for one man, a part time guide. In the area surrounding the entrance, there are a series of mosaics of Holy Mary in shaded colonnade with one donated by Ireland.

Leaving Nazareth behind, we headed north. On the way we took a small detour up a very minor road and came to an entrance with a kiosk staffed by two nuns who quickly let us through. We arrived at, for me, the most serene place of our entire journey so far – The Mount of the Beatitudes. It is on the Korazim Plateau, and it is believed that here, Jesus delivered his Sermon on the Mount.

Mt. Beatitudes

Pilgrims singing together

All around us we found extracts from the Sermon carved on low white slabs. At the age of 31, Jesus is reported to have climbed into a mountain with his disciples following him and there he delivered his sermon called The Beatitudes:

'Blessed are the poor in spirit: for theirs is the kingdom of heaven

Blessed are they that mourn: for they shall be comforted.

Blessed are the meek: for they shall inherit the earth.

Blessed are they which do hunger and thirst after righteousness: for they shall be filled.

Blessed are the merciful: for they shall obtain mercy.

Blessed are the pure in heart: for they shall see God.

Blessed are the peacemakers: for they shall be called the children of God.

Blessed are they which are persecuted for righteousness' sake: for theirs is the kingdom of heaven.'

We then came to an oratory, designed by the Italian architect Antonio Barluzzi, with windows overlooking Lake Galilee and further onto the Golan Heights. From under a tented shelter, we could hear singing. Beside a large tree, there was a group of religious pilgrims from Indonesia, perhaps 30 people altogether, in full voice. The singing was cheerful, full of rhythm and positivity, enough to get us clapping and tapping our feet. It was magical to listen to the voices, wafting on the light breeze in the afternoon sun in this serene and tranquil place.

On to Capharnaum, passing a sign for Cana (of marriage feast fame) on the way.

Capharnaum was the town the adult Jesus was very familiar with. Again, the local tourist signage was most helpful: *'Capharnaum (Capernaum) was the thriving town on the northwest shore of the Sea of Galilee, where many events in the earthly life and public ministry of Jesus Christ took place, Jesus chose five Apostles from Capharnaum; fishermen Simon (Peter), Andrew, James and John, and the tax collector Matthew. He performed many miracles here, notably the healing of the paralytic lowered through the roof of Peter's house, and the feeding of the five thousand with just a few loaves and fishes.'*

Re-discovered in the late nineteenth century, the site of Capharnaum was acquired by the Franciscan Friars of the Custody of the Holy Land in 1894. Throughout the twentieth century, friar archaeologists excavated and brought to light again, many of the ancient ruins of this Holy Place, including the house of St. Peter.

Because of their work and guardianship, it is possible for us today to visit the place where Jesus spent most of his time while here on earth.

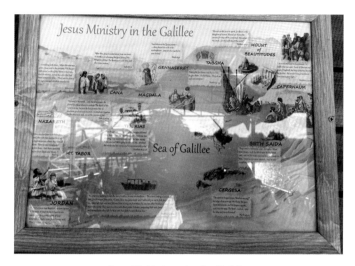

Jesus' Ministry in the Galilee

The Latin spelling *Capharnaum* is used by the Franciscan Friars and another church, built over the ruins of St Peter's house. It is a splendid, simple but impressive glass church. It is cantilevered over the ruins and has a transparent tempered glass floor. 'Upon this rock (Peter) I will build my church,' immediately came to my mind.

We visited the various ruins including the partially restored ruins of the old synagogue.

Back in the car, it's now time to eat. We stopped at the Lebanese and Galilee Restaurant. The menu featured items such as St Peter's Fish, or the Lebanese house specialities – Shanklish goat milk labnet, Eggplant, Haloumi cheese, Mujadara lentils, Fatayer green herbs and Mozayek chicken shawarma and lots more. We had a meal of Lebanese specialties.

On the wall was a large sign PEACE, over an enclosed glass case housing two fearsome spears.

We quickly followed in the footsteps of our hosts; we knew we had to make the 5.30pm departure to join a chartered Sea of Galilee boat trip. On the way we noticed hundreds of cars parked near the lakeshore. It turned out to be a special gathering of off duty armed forces, reserves and serving military, quietly gathered to commemorate and honour colleagues who had recently perished in Gaza.

We couldn't visit the Yigal Allon Centre with Man in the Galilee Exhibition and the Ancient Galilee Boat. It was closed. The Galilee boat, also known as The Jesus Boat, was discovered in 1986. It is 2,000 years old and therefore typical of the boats in the time of Jesus. The building was draped in Israeli white and blue banners, and we noted a special monument marking the garden, *A JOINT CREATION BY ARAB AND JEWISH STUDENTS.*

We hurried down the wooden marina onto a boat called, Noah, made in the style from the time of the Apostles. Already on board was the happy group we had met earlier on the Hill of the Beatitudes. The boat slipped down the mooring and out onto the lake. On one side, the Golan Heights, on the other shore by a small copse of trees, the military commemorations. While on board, the Indonesian national anthem was sung as the country's flag was hoisted on the prow. Our fellow passengers sang, prayed and danced as we clapped along. A joyous contrast.

Praise the Lord.

Raising the Indonesian flag on the Sea of Galilee

Denis sat beside a portly man wearing a red turban, when he heard that Denis was single, he immediately told him he had two eligible daughters back in Indonesia. We all hugged, shook hands and parted back on the shore.

Last stop of the day was the city of Tiberias and our overnight hotel. This time we were staying in the circular nine stories Lake Hotel, set on its own grounds, with swimming pools, tennis courts and playgrounds. It was closed to normal guests. The Israeli government had taken it over, along with many others in the area, to house displaced Israelis from the Lebanon border. Over 100,000 people had been evacuated from the northern border areas since October 7th when the Iranian-backed and supplied Hezbollah group fired rockets into Israel, in support of Hamas in the south. Our adjoining rooms were on the third floor with balconies facing the lake and the Golan Heights on the eastern shore. In the entrance hall were rails of donated new and second-hand clothing for the guests with families and older people.

Dinner was institutionally basic with a buffet and no alcohol. The hotel services had adapted to cater for its long-stay guests. These refugees in their own country were mainly rural dwellers and older. Many were clearly uncomfortable in these surroundings. They were mostly dressed in black with sticks, walkers, crutches and wheelchairs.

Sign at the hotel

A modern day disciple

Denis's thoughts:

Visiting Mt Beatitudes

The trip to Nazareth and the Sea of Galilee was very special. I had visited the area in 2016, but had not visited Mt Beatitudes. It was a place of sublimely serene peace and beauty. Seeing joyful pilgrims from India and Vietnam and Indonesia reminded me of the power of faith around the world to guide us and shape how we live and love down through the centuries, and still now. It was moving to see what these Biblical places mean to people. And it was moving to be here with Dad and Moshe and Tirza sharing friendship and reading those timeless words which have lit the way for so many people from every country in the world.

With Moshe at Mt. Beatitudes

Meeting a visitor from India

Waiting for the school bus

Day 7 (May 7th)

It was a crisp sunny morning. The Sea of Galilee was shimmering in the sunlight. In The distance the haze was lifting to reveal the beautiful Golan Heights. You could almost imagine you were in Killarney or the Lake District.

Before breakfast, I set off for a walk along the lake shore. On the way back a group of teenage Hasidic kids were waiting for the school bus. They were all dressed in black hats with white tassel shirts. They were kicking a ball and messing as teenagers do anywhere.

After breakfast Moshe mentioned, 'Tirza grew up in a village near here. It would be nice to visit her village on our way.'

Back in the car we veered to the right up into the hills overlooking the Sea of Galilee and the Jordan Valley. We stopped for photographs. Then we entered the small village of Poria Elite. 'This is where I grew up,' Tirza indicated, showing us the house, her brothers' home and also stopping at the synagogue. 'My father, the eldest of four boys, Reuban Ben-Dori, was a farmer with one helper. He was also an entrepreneur. He bought cinema projection equipment and had a mobile cinema business showing films in the surrounding area.' On the hill in front of her brother's house she went on to explain, 'There is the Golan Heights, that area was part of Syria and over there was Jordan. When I was growing up these were all mixed settlements.'

It was now getting warm, with a slight breeze on the hillside. The lake shimmered below the green fields in the Jordan valley. At the base of the Golan Heights were hectares of glasshouses. It was peaceful and eerily normal. Life continues. It was mid-morning on the 7th of May.

Our flight, KL0462, was scheduled to depart at 16.25pm. In the back of the car, I was beginning to feel anxious. 'Believe in our hosts', I reminded myself. They never missed a beat in over a week.

Apartments in Tel Aviv

Seafront in Tel Aviv

Driving south at Kinnernet we passed signs for the HaMoshava Museum, which tells the story of the first 50-years of the colony. It illustrates the lifestyle of the early settlers. Further on as we followed the road to Tel Aviv there were signs for Tye and for Haifa. As you arrive at Tel Aviv from the north, immediately you notice all the high-rise buildings. It is redeveloping itself as a modern high rise coastal city. In reality, it's just a suburb of the ancient port and city of Jaffa which is only seven kilometres away. The older part of Tel Aviv is dominated by hundreds of cranes and new construction is everywhere. The owners of older buildings are now mandated by the city administration to opt to demolish or totally rebuild and refurbish them to current environmental standards.

Described by the New York Times as the Mediterranean Capital of Cool, Tel Aviv with a population of over 500,000, is a city with a savvy attitude and cultural astuteness. The city which never sleeps, is a centre for nightlife, cuisine, culture and liberalism – according to the Israeli Tourist board. It is also the commercial, tech and business centre of Israel.

Driving along the long seafront with its beaches, cafes, umbrellas, palm trees, boardwalks and cycle paths, it reminded me of perhaps a Barcelona in the making. The traffic was heavy with many Google diversions to avoid colossal road and construction works. We passed the Opera House and then the glass curtain-walled library, still trying to function in the middle of demonstrations. Adjacent is the square where, as we see in our TVs at home, nightly protest rallies take place, overlooked by an enormous banner stating *#BringThemHome*.

#BringThemHome Banner   *Tamar & Yoram Metzger*

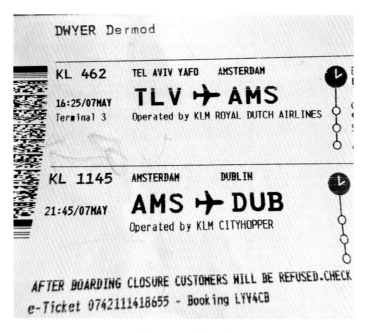

Homeward Bound

30 minutes later we are pulling into the front of Tel Aviv's Ben Gurion International Airport. Moshe has made a call to his friend, the Airport CEO. We are met, assigned a dedicated executive/sherpa to manage us through check-in and past security to a VIP lane. Within 20-minutes of arriving we are airside and in the departures lounge. In all my time in the travel industry, I have never experienced such a smooth politeness and efficient exit from a country.

The airport is practically empty with very few flights in or out.

On the way to our departure gates, hundreds of individual pictures of those who died or are prisoners are emblazoned on the sides of the glass travelators.

In the airport shop, The Jerusalem Post headline is:

> *'Hamas says accepts ceasefire; Israel mulls terms. Sub headlines are: Deal has elements Jerusalem can't accept. War cabinet sends teams for talks.'*

We passed a coffee shop called Moses Airlines. A forty-year odyssey perhaps

Our flight to Schiphol is full, mainly with Hasidic/Orthodox Jewish men and their families. I assume many are returning to their diamond and related businesses in Amsterdam and Antwerp. Our onward connection to Dublin on KL 1145 was less busy. We landed after midnight on May 8th and we were met by my wife, Helen, and our new rescue dog, a Cocker Spaniel named Sandy.

We were away for 23 days, driven over 3,500 kilometres and flown 7,930 kilometres. We experienced no delays and thankfully had no accidents. We saw remarkable places, met incredibly hospitable courageous people and witnessed on the ground the direct and indirect effects of an expanding horrific, turbulent war.

Dad meeting Sandy

Denis arrives home to Ted &
Tigger

POSTSCRIPT

Some weeks before we left in mid-April, I heard the spokeperson for Iran on the radio. In response to a tough question from the Irish news anchor, he said: 'You [in the West] are in the cinema just now – commenting in the middle of an unfinished movie that started over 75 years ago.'

Maybe he is right. We can only recount the 22-day slice of the movie that we journeyed through.

Before we left Israel, I went to one of the H Stern jewellery stores to buy a present to bring home to Helen. I had the large shop to myself. Finally, I picked a suitable piece, agreed on the price and as the lady was wrapping it and preparing the credit card machine, her boss, the store manager came over. 'Welcome. Where are you from?' he asked. 'Dublin,' I responded. 'Oh, that must be terrible – you are having such an awful time there – riots, immigrants, fires, stabbings and the universities closed. We see it nightly on our screens.' And as an afterthought she added 'the situation is much quieter here.'

What more can you say?

A couple of days after we returned to Ireland – a WhatsApp message arrived from Tirza and Moshe:

> *'Thanks for being open minded to the complexity of the situation here and your prayers. Denis is honest and sincere, good questions to each one of them!!! Not that I know all the answers and if they are the right ones. Because not always there is right or wrong. But God is our witness (whoever he/she is) that we are trying very hard to do the right things. And to see and try to understand the point of view of the other side (even though it might be cruel and devastating). Again, thank you for your passion to learn and trying to understand the complicated*

situation. Regarding Helen, the fact that she supported you in this amazing venture is wonderful. Big hug from the promised land.'

My niece messaged us:

'I can stand down my worry-ometer now! What an amazing experience.'

On May 28th, just three weeks after we returned, the Irish government issued a statement:

> *At a meeting of the government today (May 28, 2024) Ireland formally recognised the State of Palestine.*
>
> *The Government recognises Palestine as a sovereign and independent state and agreed to establish full diplomatic relations between Dublin and Ramallah.*
>
> *An Ambassador of Ireland to the State of Palestine will be appointed along with a full Embassy of Ireland in Ramallah. (On 11, 2024 Ireland formally appointed Jilan Wahba Abdalmajid as Ireland's first ambassador to the State of Palestine.)*
>
> *The Government noted the tragic backdrop to today's announcement and again called for an immediate ceasefire in Gaza, the release of Israeli hostages and unhindered access for humanitarian aid.*
>
> *Ireland recognises the State of Palestine in the spirit of peace in a coordinated announcement with our friends and colleagues in Spain and Norway.*
>
> *A UN special committee has said that Israeli policies and practices in Gaza are 'consistent with the characteristics of genocide'.*
>
> *The committee, set up in 1968 to monitor the Israeli occupation, also said in its annual report that there were serious concerns that Israel was 'using starvation as a weapon of war' in the 13-month-old conflict, and was running an 'apartheid system' in the West Bank, including East Jerusalem.*

The Guardian Thu 14 Nov 2024 17.01 CET

Denis adds:

January 6 2025 (Nollaig na mBan)

The day before this book goes to print, Bono – a hero of mine and many others – was awarded the Presidential Medal of Freedom by President Joe Biden. In thanks for this honour, and in order to discuss the evolving meanings of the concept of 'freedom', he penned an article for The Atlantic Monthly on 4 January in which he articulated superbly how many people feel, us included. Here is a short excerpt:

> *And then there's Gaza. Israel's prime minister for almost 20 years, Benjamin Netanyahu, has often used the defense of Israel's freedom and its people as an excuse to systematically deny the same freedom and security to the Palestinians – a self-defeating and deadly contradiction, which has led to an obscene leveling of civilian life that the world can visualize daily on their cellphones. Freedom must come for the Israeli hostages, whose kidnapping by Hamas ignited this latest cataclysm. Freedom must come for the Palestinian people. It does not take a prophet to predict Israel will never be free until Palestine is free.*

15 December 2024: Israel closes its embassy in Ireland/ Palestinian Ambassador appointed in Dublin

As we completed our account of our visit to this region with a long and troubled history amid renewed talk of a ceasefire in Gaza, diplomatic relations between Israel and Ireland took a downturn with Israel deciding to shut its embassy in Dublin. The Israeli Foreign Minister Gideon Sa'ar announced the closure citing the *"extreme anti-Israel policy of the Irish government. The antisemitic actions and rhetoric that Ireland is taking against Israel are based on delegitimization and demonization of the Jewish state and on double standards,"* said Sa'ar in a statement. *"Ireland has crossed all red lines in its relationship with Israel."*

Irish Prime Minister Simon Harris called the decision *"deeply regrettable. I utterly reject the assertion that Ireland is anti-Israel,"* Harris wrote on X following Sa'ar's announcement. *"Ireland is pro-peace, pro-human rights and pro-international law. Ireland wants a two-state solution and for Israel and Palestine to live in peace and security. Ireland will always speak up for human rights and international law,"* he added.

Two days later Irish President Michael D Higgins called the remarks by the Israeli Foreign Minister *'deep slander'*. Irish news service The Journal reported that at a ceremony at Áras an Uachtaráin where the Palestinian Ambassador was appointed – a formality that is part of Ireland recognising Palestinian statehood – Higgins said it was a "historic" and "great" day. *"I think it's very important to express, as President of Ireland, to say that the Irish people are antisemitic is a deep slander,"* Higgins said. *"To suggest because one criticises Prime Minister Netanyahu that one is antisemitic is such a gross defamation and slander."*

Hamas and Netanyahu – 'fake news' or unholy bedfellows?

During our time in Israel we were told by more than one Israeli, and by more than one Palestinian, that Hamas had been supported in its rise by Israeli Prime Minister Benjamin Netanyahu and others around him, and that it seemed impossible that his security services had no knowledge of the impending attacks on 7 October. Netanyahu of course is on trial for corruption & bribery charges since 2020 *(despite years of delaying tactics, he was finally forced to take the stand in court on 10 December 2024)*. The military and political coalition which he leads includes a number of people from the very far right of Israeli ideology – with a diverse set of religious & military aims – many of which are at odds with the will of the majority of Israelis. Could Netanyahu really have supported the rise of Hamas? I looked this up and found articles published in respected mainstream media outlets, both Israeli and international, supportive of this view.

Headline from The Times of Israel, 8 October 2023:

For years, Netanyahu propped up Hamas. Now it's blown up in our faces

> *"The premier's policy of treating the terror group as a partner, at the expense of Abbas and Palestinian statehood, has resulted in wounds that will take Israel years to heal from"*

From The Nation Magazine, December 11th 2023:

> *The same is true of Netanyahu's long standing policy of bolstering Hamas rule in Gaza, including encouraging Israel's de facto ally Qatar to finance the terrorist organisation. While the much-respected Israeli newspaper Haaretz has covered this issue, it has been largely ignored by the international press.*

> *On Sunday, The New York Times gave new prominence to the long-standing Netanyahu-Hamas connection in a detailed and lengthy report. According to the newspaper: Just weeks before Hamas launched the deadly Oct. 7 attacks on Israel, the head of Mossad arrived in Doha, Qatar, for a meeting with Qatari officials. For years, the Qatari government had been sending millions of dollars a month into the Gaza Strip – money that helped prop up the Hamas government there. Prime Minister Benjamin Netanyahu of Israel not only tolerated those payments, he had encouraged them.*

> *According to the Times, Israeli intelligence agents travelled into Gaza with a Qatari official carrying suitcases filled with cash to disperse money. Retired Israeli general Shlomo Brom described the logic of Netanyahu's position: "One effective way to prevent a two-state solution is to divide between the Gaza Strip and the West Bank." If the extremist Hamas-ruled Gaza, then the Palestinian Authority – a compromised communist government with a tenuous hold on the West Bank – would be further weakened. This, according to Brom, would allow Netanyahu to say: "I have no partner".*

From Associated Press, 1 December 2023:

JERUSALEM (AP) – Israel's military was aware of Hamas' plan to launch an attack on Israeli soil over a year before the devastating Oct. 7 operation that killed hundreds of people, The New York Times reported Friday.

It was the latest in a series of signs that top Israeli commanders either ignored or played down warnings that Hamas was plotting the attack, which triggered a war against the Islamic militant group that has devastated the Gaza Strip.

Dermod adds:

While thinking about what to share in this postscript, a friend we met in Jerusalem sent us the following email. The content seems to sum up the present situation and the future outlook. One can only hope they are wrong. The email said:

'I re-read a short letter that the Latin Patriarch Cardinal Pizza Bella sent to his Churches in the Holy Land on August 9. I am sure it was not an easy letter to write since it is impossible to put the present situation in words.

'Many months have now passed since the beginning of this terrible war. The suffering caused by this conflict and the dismay at what is happening are not only unabated but seem to be fuelled again and again by hatred, resentment, and contempt, which only intensify the violence and push away the possibility of finding solutions. Indeed, it is becoming increasingly difficult to envision a conclusion to this conflict, whose impact on the lives of our people is greater and more painful than ever before. It is becoming increasingly difficult to find people and institutions with whom a dialog about the future and peaceful relations is possible. We all seem to be crushed by this present, which is characterised by so much violence and, admittedly, anger.

'The Patriarch describes a grim reality and begs the question of how we can sustain hope when confronted with this reality. Reflecting on this, it came to me that if our reality is our truth, then we are pretty much doomed. We might as well give up, and there definitely is the temptation to do so.'

Denis's concluding thoughts:

What the trip taught me is that these countries and peoples have influenced everyone in the world through the evolution of faith, trade, languages and civilisation, and the region's past and present continues to resonate and reverberate around the globe. It became apparent to me that the situation in the region is far more complicated and complex than I had understood before visiting. Every layer of history or incident when examined reveals another layer from another viewpoint which makes it difficult to draw any fixed conclusions or have any certain opinions. For too many people, history remains a nightmare from which they cannot yet wake up.

I found myself quite sad for weeks after coming home from all we had heard from people from various perspectives and faiths. We had listened to and empathised with those we met from all sides, and the pain and suffering of many people was palpable. But the kindness of people everywhere is also what stood out. Shared food, smiles, laughter, handshakes, hugs, good wishes.

Beyond the violence and the noise of the extremists and warmakers, if one has the chance to see them, there are so many inspiring pockets of coexistence and co-operation which offer hope for a better shared future – bubbles of sanity in a sea of madness. My hope is that there is always hope – hope that over time more people will take time to listen and understand each other's history and culture and in so doing better understand their shared humanity and recognise that they have far more in common than that which divides them. Most people just want peace and the chance to create opportunities for their families.

There is a quote by filmmaker Albert Maysles: 'tyranny is the deliberate removal of nuance'. Everything in this region is deeply nuanced, and it is important for those who wish to work as peacemakers, and for those who wish to help reconstruct and offer economic opportunity in the Levant, to take the time to understand the nuances in order to be able to work productively with and across all communities. The past and the future of the world, and the past and the future of the Levant, are inextricably linked. Isn't it in everyone's interests to work towards solutions with those who are interested in solutions.

Finally, it truly hit home to me how lucky many of us are here in Ireland all things considered. It wasn't always this way, so it's worth taking time sometimes to count our blessings. And the trip with my adventurous Dad reminded me of just how blessed we are. And how lucky I am to have been able to take this trip with him.

Karshi Jerusalem 1955 silver orb gift from Tirza and Moshe.

'On one of those days of never-ending war, I received a surprising call from Ireland. On the line was my longtime friend Dermod Dwyer. We had met several times over forty years in America, Paris, Lisbon, Jordan, and also in Ireland on various occasions. That's what I recall. We were fortunate to stay at his house and get to know Helen. At the time, I thought what a waste for him, if he had operated in a more central and peaceful place in the world and not in a country accompanied by struggles... Ireland. Years ago, Dermod promised me he would come to Jerusalem, 'The Promised Land.' An Irish gentleman will keep his promise, even after forty years. In the brief conversation, Dermod said that his son Denis and he planned to travel to

Krak des Chevaliers, the Crusader fortress in Syria, and visited Jerusalem, Jordan, and Lebanon. He also stated that he was very much looking forward to this trip.

I immediately imagined him being questioned and researched for hours at the entrance to Israel or other Arab countries he mentioned. After the short conversation, Tirza asked me if I understood why now. I didn't reply, but I added that I would be happy to help. In the footsteps of Lawrence, I thought immediately, and I turned with quite an effort, climbing to my beloved library that I hadn't visited in a long time. That was to find two books. Fortunately, I found them immediately. The first book was Seven Pillars of Wisdom. The second, much less-known book, was Lawrence's master's thesis on Crusader fortresses. This is also one of Lawrence's many secrets. Lawrence of Arabia, I smiled to myself, the most admired Arabist, was one of the great supporters of the Zionist movement and an admirer of Jewish activity in Israel.

It was very clear to me that the decision of Dermod and his son to come to the area was brave. We continued planning their itinerary, discussing their safety (mainly with Helen). I gave them some addresses of my contacts in countries defined as enemies to Israel, who could help in case of trouble, and of good people and reliable service providers. I tried to see what would be most interesting for them. I treated their travel to be a pilgrimage to Jerusalem (Holy Land) as if it were my trip with my sons, trying to introduce my beloved, beautiful country and its history, not ignoring the complexity of the tragic conflicts on the one hand, as Joyce expressed it in Ulysses: 'History is a nightmare from which I am trying to awake,' but at the same time remembering Ben Gurion's quote: 'A nation that does not respect its past has no future,' and the revolutions and innovations that have taken place here on any scale for the last 3,000 years. I hope that my love for this bloody, painful, and complex land, but at the same time caressing and embracing land and all its people and their history, has passed on to my friends and my children.'

Tirza

'I grew up in Peoria Elit (a village in the lower Galilee). My father's name was Reuben Ben-Dori (In Germany his original family name was Laufer and first name Hans). When he immigrated to Israel, he changed his family name to Ben-Dori which means in Hebrew the son of my generation and his first name to Reuben which was the eldest son of Jacob (he was the eldest son of the 4 boys in his family). Thanks for being interested.'

And finally.

Our father-and-son trip was truly unforgettable – an odyssey in every sense. I can't express how lucky and privileged we both feel to have shared this experience. We witnessed the journey together, each seeing it through our own unique perspectives, hearing it with different ears and remembering it in our own distinct ways. And through it all, I knew he had my back.

ACKNOWLEDGEMENTS

This book began with a burst of amateur enthusiasm and effort, before crashing with the realisation that a substandard travel journal stream of consciousness wouldn't cut it. Hopefully the final version is better. It is our genuine best effort, in the aftermath of the two of us getting back home to pick up the pieces of our own normality. We saw and experienced our odyssey differently and this book clearly demonstrates that.

So many people have helped. Some brought grounded common sense to expectations. All to offer practical help, advice, and join with us to make sense of this journey.

Never having written a book together, we are so grateful to the following for guiding, goading and getting us there.

Our two editors – Yvonne Reddin as copy editor, and Peter Murtagh, as a friend and guiding editor – and our superb designer Eimear D'Arcy.

Our publisher, Orla Kelly, a Cork lady, who herself has learned the hard way of publishing and now professionally guides so many aspiring writers to make their dreams a publishing reality. We certainly learned about the route to traditional publishing. It is thorough, painstaking, time consuming and slow. Ordinarily we might have chosen that route, and we were offered introductions to major Irish publishers. Because of the subject matter and our belief in the 'perishability' and current 'high profile' of the region – we have chosen a hybrid publishing model. Hopefully it will work.

Without the professional help of Kate Archer, Untamed Borders and the DMC Golden Target Tourism and Travel team on the ground, without whom we could not have travelled to Syria in the first place. They arranged everything, entry visas, hotels, Jusuf our driver, Taysir our guide, and all the entry fees. For the Syrian segment of our journey, we were so blessed to join Erin and Francesca. Each one is amazing. Together they were awesome, witty and just the best travel companions.

We clicked. At very short notice Atlas Travel. Amman looked after our ground arrangements in Jordan, including our guide Amer, driver and hotels. Moshe and Tirza Hananel, arranged just about everything in Israel including the visit to the wall/gates of Gaza with Dr. Ron and Dr. Yudithe Lobel and our invitation to the annual Yad Vashem Holocaust remembrance. They also introduced us to our guides, Martin Goldberg and Ibrahim Ghazzawi.

His book would not be here without the endless patience and skilful help of my wife Helen. In other ways we are grateful for the encouragement of Frank Cronin, David Harvey, Peter Murtagh, William Micklem, and to our neighbour Susan Walkin for SOS technical assistance at very short notice! In early 1995 without the encouragement of my colleague Noel Sweeney, I would never have had the opportunity to travel to the Middle East. We are grateful to Darren Benett, *dkb creative* for the wonderful bespoke maps of the region and Jerusalem. And to Sarah Hutch for tuition on the use of the iPhone camera.

Denis adds:

I would like to thank all of the guides who gave us such an amazing insight into their countries (Albert, Hassane, Taysir, Amer, Martin and Ibrahim). I am hugely grateful to Moshe, Tirza, Yuval, Erin & Fran for their kindness and friendship, and special thanks to my friends Annie and Sahoko for kindly looking after Ted and Tigger while I was away. I'm very appreciative of all of the efforts of those Dad has listed above who helped to bring the book to life (especially Orla, Yvonne, Eimear and Peter). And I'm very thankful to Dad and Helen for all they do for me and for others. And to Cal and Mum for watching over me – miss and love you always.

I'd like to express my sympathy to all those who have lost loved ones through these terrible conflicts. May they find the strength to keep going. I'd finally like to express my heartfelt admiration for the peacemakers of the world, for all of those who speak truth to power, and for those who strive to see the good in everyone regardless of creed, race, nationality, gender or sexual orientation. May there be better days ahead. There is always hope.

ABOUT THE AUTHORS

Dermod Dwyer is a prominent figure in Ireland's hospitality and tourism industry. He began his career in 1968 and has held significant roles, including Executive Chairman of The Convention Centre Dublin (CCD) from 1997 to 2021. Dwyer was instrumental in the CCD's development, overseeing its design, construction, and successful operation. He serves as Chairman of Powerscourt Estate and Gardens and also served as Chairman of Setanta Sports Broadcasting Ireland. Additionally, he co-founded the Caroline Foundation for Cancer Research with his wife Helen, and has been involved with various educational and cultural institutions in Ireland.

Denis Dwyer is a film producer who has worked on the award-winning documentaries 'Abbeyfealegood' (2019) and 'The Irish Pub' (2013). 'Abbeyfealegood', directed by Alex Fegan, explores themes of love, loss, and life through the stories of barbers and hairdressers in Abbeyfeale, County Limerick. Denis has also been involved in other projects like 'Patricia' and 'Face Values,' which focus on visual artists. In 2008 he and five friends cycled 12.500 miles from Cairo to Cape Town, raising funds for healthcare and education projects through Millennium Promise. His career includes roles in marketing and recruitment.